Alan Jacobs is president of the Ramana Maharshi Foundation U.K. He has made a lifelong study of mysticism and is the author of many books, including *Poetic Transcreations of the Principal Upanishads*, *The Bhagavad Gita* and *The Gnostic Gospels*. He has compiled the anthologies *Poetry for the Spirit* and *Peace of Mind*. As a poet, he is the author of two collections, *Myrobalan of the Magi* and *Mastering Music Walks the Sunlit Sea*. Amongst other books, he has written *When Jesus Lived in India* and a novella, *Eutopia*. He lives in London.

GANDHI

Radical Wisdom for a Changing World

WATKINS PUBLISHING

LONDON

This edition first published in the UK and USA 2012 by
Watkins Publishing, Sixth Floor, Castle House,
75–76 Wells Street, London W1T 3QH

Extracts from material kindly supplied with permission by the
Bombay Sarvadaya Mandal and Gandhi Research Foundation.

Design and typesetting copyright © Watkins Publishing 2012
Biographical essay and compilation and selection of text
copyright © Alan Jacobs 2012

1 3 5 7 9 10 8 6 4 2

Designed and typeset by Jerry Goldie Graphic Design

Printed in India

British Library Cataloguing-in-Publication Data Available
Library of Congress Cataloging-in-Publication Data Available

ISBN: 978-1-78028-126-1

www.watkinspublishing.co.uk

Distributed in the USA and Canada by Sterling Publishing Co., Inc.
387 Park Avenue South, New York, NY 10016-8810

For information about custom editions, special sales, premium and
corporate purchases, please contact Sterling Special Sales
Department at 800-805-5489 or specialsales@sterlingpub.com

Contents

ACKNOWLEDGEMENT

With grateful thanks and appreciation to the Publication Division, Government of India, New Delhi, for *The Collected Works of Mahatma Gandhi*. Without the publication of the 98 volumes recording the Mahatma's letters, speeches and writings, thus placing them in the public domain, this anthology would not have been possible.

With thanks to Alison Bolus for her invaluable editorial assistance.

Introduction

'In the attitude of silence the soul finds the path in a clearer light, and what is elusive and deceptive resolves itself into crystal clearness. Our life is a long and arduous quest after Truth.'

Mahatma Gandhi

I n endeavouring to compile an anthology on the life and wisdom of one of the greatest men who have ever lived on planet Earth, Mahatma Gandhi, I decided in Part 1, after a biography of sorts (mostly extracts from his autobiography) of this almost unprecedented hero of a nation, to try to paint an impressive portrait of his struggles and spiritual views by drawing on a selection of extracts from his own *Collected Works*, which comprise one hundred volumes. I have selected key passages from letters, speeches, writings and interviews in these volumes, which, when put together, draw a graphic picture of what this great soul endured and achieved in his momentous life, before he was tragically killed by the bullet of a fanatic assassin.

The extracts I have selected are chronological and start with the preparatory period for his great historic role in his South African days, as a young lawyer fighting to protect the rights of the persecuted Indian minority in that country. Then we move to his decision to return and study conditions in his beloved India, having made the crucial decision to work with great determination for the liberation of India from the long domination of British Imperial rule.

His method was totally revolutionary in the sense that, although it was a political aim, he was inspired by ancient spiritual values drawn from the noble religious heritage of Hinduism. Thus, non-violence, strong faith and strict rules of ethical conduct inspired his life, and after an heroic and almost single-handed struggle, he achieved his aim.

In Part 2, I have chosen a selection of memorable quotations that best illustrate his moral and spiritual vision.

Bapu, as he was affectionately nicknamed by his people, became known after Independence as the father of his people, and became a heroic role model for all Indians endeavouring to lead a religious life. 'Mahatma' means 'great soul', and this epithet undoubtedly applies to this unique God-Man, who was totally surrendered to the Higher Being externally and intimately in his heart. I trust the anthology will achieve its aim of giving the reader an impressive overview of the life and struggle of the Mahatma in an easily accessible form.

Alan Jacobs
President, Ramana Maharshi Foundation UK
London, 2011

Biography of
Mohandas
Karamchand Gandhi

with extracts from *An Autobiography*

The Gandhis belonged to the Bania caste and seem to have been originally grocers. But for three generations, from my grandfather, they have been Prime Ministers in several Kathiawad States. Uttamchand Gandhi, alias Ota Gandhi, my grandfather, must have been a man of principle. State intrigues compelled him to leave Porbandar, where he was Diwan, and to seek refuge in Junagadh. There he saluted the Nawab with the left hand. Someone, noticing the apparent discourtesy, asked for an explanation, which was given thus: 'The right hand is already pledged to Porbandar.'

Ota Gandhi married a second time, having lost his first wife. He had four sons by his first wife and two by his second wife. I do not think that in my childhood I ever felt or knew that these sons of Ota Gandhi were not all of the same mother. The fifth of these six brothers was Karamchand Gandhi, alias Kaba Gandhi, and the sixth was Tulsidas

Gandhi. Both these brothers were Prime Ministers in Porbandar, one after the other. Kaba Gandhi was my father. He was a member of the Rajasthanik Court. It is now extinct, but in those days it was a very influential body for settling disputes between the chiefs and their fellow clansmen. He was for some time Prime Minister in Rajkot and then in Vankaner. He was a pensioner of the Rajkot State when he died.

Kaba Gandhi married four times in succession, having lost his wife each time by death. He had two daughters by his first and second marriages. His last wife, Putlibai, bore him a daughter and three sons, I being the youngest.

My father was a lover of his clan, truthful, brave and generous, but short-tempered. To a certain extent he might have been given to carnal pleasures. For he married for the fourth time when he was over forty. But he was incorruptible and had earned a name for strict impartiality in his family as well as outside. His loyalty to the state was well known. An Assistant Political Agent spoke insultingly of the Rajkot Thakore Saheb, his chief, and he stood up to the insult. The agent was angry and asked Kaba Gandhi to apologize. This he refused to do and was therefore kept under detention for a few hours. But when the agent saw that Kaba Gandhi was adamant, he ordered him to be released.

My father never had any ambition to accumulate riches and left us very little property.

He had no education, save that of experience. At best, he might be said to have read up to the fifth Gujarati standard. Of history and geography he was innocent. But his rich experience of practical affairs stood him in good stead in the solution of the most intricate questions and in managing hundreds of men. Of religious training he had very little, but he had that kind of religious culture that frequent visits to temples and listening to religious discourses make available to many Hindus. In his last days he began reading the *Gita* at the instance of a learned Brahman friend of the family, and he used to repeat aloud some verses every day at the time of worship.

The outstanding impression my mother has left on my memory is that of saintliness. She was deeply religious. She would not think of taking her meals without her daily prayers. Going to Haveli – the Vaishnava temple – was one of her daily duties. As far as my memory can go back, I do not remember her having ever missed the Chaturmas [a four-month period of penance and observing vows, such as silence, fasting or abstaining from certain foods]. She would take the hardest vows and keep them without flinching. Illness was no excuse for relaxing them. I can recall her once falling ill when she was observing the Chandrayana vow [a religious fast], but the illness was not allowed to interrupt the observance. To keep two or three consecutive fasts was nothing to her. Living on one meal a day during Chaturmas was a habit with her. Not content with that, she fasted every alternate day during one Chaturmas. During another Chaturmas, she vowed not to have food without seeing the sun. We children on those days would stand, staring at the sky, waiting to announce the appearance of the sun to our mother. Everyone knows that at the height of the rainy season the sun often does not condescend to show his face. And I remember days when, at his sudden appearance, we would rush and announce it to her, She would run out to see with her own eyes, but by that time the fugitive sun would be gone, thus depriving her of her meal. 'That does not matter,' she would say cheerfully, 'God did not want me to eat today.' And then she would return to her round of duties.

My mother had strong commonsense. She was well informed about all matters of state, and ladies of the court thought highly of her intelligence. Often I would accompany her, exercising the privilege of childhood, and I still remember many lively discussions she had with the widowed mother of the Thakore Saheb.

Of these parents I was born at Porbandar, otherwise known as Sudamapuri, on the 2nd October 1869. I passed my childhood in Porbandar. I recollect having been put to school. It was with some difficulty that I got through the multiplication tables. The fact that I recollect nothing more of those days than having learnt, in company with other boys, to call our teacher all kinds of names, would strongly suggest that my intellect must have been sluggish, and my memory raw.

I must have been about seven when my father left Porbandar for Rajkot to become a member of the Rajasthanik Court. There I was put into a primary school, and I can well recollect those days, including the names and other particulars of the teachers who taught me. As at Porbandar, so here, there is hardly anything to note about my studies. I could only have been a mediocre student. From this school I went to the suburban school and thence to the high school, having already reached my twelfth year. I do not remember having ever told a lie, during this short period, either to my teachers or to my school-mates. I used to be very shy and avoided all company. My books and my lessons were my sole companions. To be at school at the stroke of the hour and to run back home as soon as the school closed – that was my daily habit. I literally ran back, because I could not bear to talk to anybody. I was even afraid lest anyone should poke fun at me.

There is an incident which occurred at the examination during my first year at the high school and which is worth recording. Mr. Giles, the educational Inspector, had come on a visit of inspection. He had set us five words to write as a spelling exercise. One of the words was 'Kettle'. I had mis-spelt it. The teacher tried to prompt me with the point of his boot, but I would not be prompted. It was beyond me to see that he wanted me to copy the spelling from my neighbor's slate, for I had thought that the teacher was there to supervise us against copying. The result was that all the boys, except myself, were found to have spelt every word correctly. Only I had been stupid. The teacher tried later to bring this stupidity home to me, but without effect. I never could learn the art of 'copying'.

Yet the incident did not in the least diminish my respect for my teacher. I was, by nature, blind to the faults of elders. Later I came to know of many other failings of this teacher, but my regard for him remained the same. For I had learnt to carry out the orders of elders, not to scan their actions.

Two other incidents belonging to the same period have always clung to my memory. As a rule I had a distaste for any reading beyond my school books. The daily lessons had to be done, because I disliked being taken to task by my teacher as much as I disliked deceiving him. Therefore I would do the lessons, but often without my mind in them. Thus when even the lessons could not be done properly, there was of course no question of any extra reading. But somehow my eyes fell on a book purchased by my father. It was *Shravana Pitribhakti Nataka* (a play about Shravana's devotion to his parents). I read it with intense interest. There came to our place about the same time itinerant showmen. One of the pictures I was shown was of Shravana carrying, by means of slings fitted for his shoulders, his blind parents on a pilgrimage. The book and the picture left an indelible impression on my mind. 'Here is an example for you to copy,' I said to myself. The agonized lament of the parents over Shravana's death is still fresh in my memory. The melting tune moved me deeply, and I played it on a concertina that my father had purchased for me.

There was a similar incident connected with another play. Just about this time, I had secured my father's permission to see a play performed by a certain dramatic company. This play – *Harishchandra* – captured my heart. I could never be tired of seeing it. But how often should I be permitted to go? It haunted me and I must have acted *Harishchandra* to myself times without number. 'Why should not all be truthful like Harishchandra?' was the question I asked myself day and night. To follow truth and to go through all the ordeals Harishchandra went through was the one ideal it inspired in me. I literally believed in the story of Harishchandra. The thought of it all often made me weep. My commonsense tells me today that Harishchandra could not have been a historical character. Still both Harishchandra and Shravana are living realities for me, and I am sure I should be moved as before if I were to read those plays again today.

Marriage at age of 13

Much as I wish that I had not to write this chapter, I know that I shall have to swallow many such bitter draughts in the course of this narrative. And I cannot do otherwise, if I claim to be a worshipper of Truth. It is my painful duty to have to record here my marriage at the age of thirteen. As I see the youngsters of the same age about me who are under my care, and think of my own marriage, I am inclined to pity myself and to congratulate them on having escaped my lot. I can see no moral argument in support of such a preposterously early marriage.

My betrothal

Let the reader make no mistake. I was married, not betrothed. For in Kathiawad there are two distinct rites – betrothal and marriage. Betrothal is a preliminary promise on the part of the parents of the boy and the girl to join them in marriage, and it is not inviolable. The death of the boy entails no widowhood on the girl. It is an agreement purely between the parents, and the children have no concern with it. Often they are not even informed of it. It appears that I was betrothed thrice, though without my knowledge. I was told that two girls chosen for me had died in turn, and therefore I infer that I was betrothed three times. I have a faint recollection, however, that the third betrothal took place in my seventh year. But I do not recollect having been informed about it. In the present chapter I am talking about my marriage, of which I have the clearest recollection.

My brothers

It will be remembered that we were three brothers. The first was already married. The elders decided to marry my second brother, who was two or three years my senior, a cousin, possibly a year older, and me, all at the same time. In doing so there was no thought of our welfare, much less our wishes. It was purely a question of their own convenience and economy.

At high school

My studies were continued. I was not regarded as a dunce at the high school. I always enjoyed the affection of my teachers. Certificates of progress and character used to be sent to the parents every year. I never had a bad certificate. In fact I even won prizes after I passed out of the second standard. In the fifth and sixth I obtained scholarships of rupees four and ten respectively, an achievement for which I have to thank good luck more than my merit. For the scholarships were not open to all, but reserved for the best boys amongst those coming from the Sorath Division of

Kathiawad. And in those days there could not have been many boys from Sorath in a class of forty to fifty.

Once receiving corporal punishment

My own recollection is that I had not any high regard for my ability. I used to be astonished whenever I won prizes and scholarships. But I very jealously guarded my character. The least little blemish drew tears from my eyes. When I merited, or seemed to the teacher to merit, a rebuke, it was unbearable for me. I remember having once received corporal punishment. I did not so much mind the punishment as the fact that it was considered my dessert. I wept piteously. That was when I was in the first or second standard. There was another such incident during the time when I was in the seventh standard. Dorabji Edulji Gimi was the headmaster then. He was popular among boys, as he was a disciplinarian, a man of method and a good teacher. He had made gymnastics and cricket compulsory for boys of the upper standards. I disliked both. I never took part in any exercise, cricket or football, before they were made compulsory. My shyness was one of the reasons for this aloofness, which I now see was wrong. I then had the false notion that gymnastics had nothing to do with education.

On exercise

I may mention, however, that I was none the worse for abstaining from exercise. That was because I had read in books about the benefits of long walks in the open air, and having liked the advice, I had formed a habit of taking walks, which has still remained with me. These walks gave me a fairly hardy constitution.

On gymnastics

The reason for my dislike for gymnastics was my keen desire to serve as nurse to my father. As soon as the school closed, I would hurry home and begin serving him. Compulsory exercise came directly in the way of this service. I requested Mr. Gimi to exempt me from gymnastics so that I might be free to serve my father. But he would not listen to me. Now it happened that one Saturday, when we had school in the morning, I had to go from home to the school for gymnastics at four o'clock in the afternoon. I had no watch, and the clouds deceived me. Before I reached the school the boys had all left. The next day Mr. Gimi, examining the roll, found me marked absent. Being asked the reason for absence, I told him what had happened. He refused to believe me and ordered me to pay a fine of one or two annas (I cannot now recall how much).

Convicted of lying

I was convicted of lying! That deeply pained me. How was I to prove my innocence? There was no way. I cried in deep anguish. I saw that a man of truth must also be a man of care. This was the first and last instance of my carelessness in school. I have a faint recollection that I finally succeeded in getting the fine remitted. The exemption from exercise was of course obtained, as my father wrote himself to the headmaster saying that he wanted me at home after school.

On bad handwriting

But though I was none the worse for having neglected exercise, I am still paying the penalty of another neglect. I do not know whence I got the notion that good handwriting was not a necessary part of education, but I retained it until I went to England. When later, especially in South Africa, I saw the beautiful handwriting of lawyers and young men born and educated in South Africa, I was ashamed of myself and repented of my neglect. I saw that bad handwriting should be regarded as a sign of an imperfect education. I tried later to improve mine, but it was too late. I could never repair the neglect of my youth. Let every young man and woman be warned by my example, and understand that good handwriting is a necessary part of education. I am now of opinion that children should first be taught the art of drawing before learning how to write. Let the child learn his letters by observation as he does different objects, such as flowers, birds etc., and let him learn handwriting only after he has learnt to draw objects. He will then write a beautifully formed hand.

School reminiscences

Two more reminiscences of my school days are worth recording. I had lost one year because of my marriage, and the teacher wanted me to make good the loss by skipping a class – a privilege usually allowed to industrious boys. I therefore had only six months in the third standard and was prompted to the forth after the examinations which are followed by the summer vacation. English became the medium of instruction in most subjects from the fourth standard. I found myself completely at sea. Geometry was a new subject in which I was not particularly strong, and the English medium made it still more difficult for me. The teacher taught the subject very well, but I could not follow him. Often I would lose heart and think of going back to the third standard, feeling that the packing of two years' studies into a single year was too ambitious. But this would discredit not only me, but also the teacher; because, counting on my industry, he had recommended my promotion. So the fear of the double discredit kept me at my post. When however, with much effort I reached the thirteenth proposition of Euclid, the utter simplicity of the subject was suddenly revealed to me. A subject which only required a pure and simple use of one's reasoning powers could not be difficult. Ever since that time geometry has been both easy and interesting for me.

Learning Samskrit

Samskrit, however, proved a harder task. In geometry there was nothing to memorize, whereas in Samskrit, I thought, everything had to be learnt by heart. This subject also was commenced from the fourth standard. As soon as I entered the sixth I became disheartened. The teacher was a hard taskmaster, anxious, as I thought, to force the boys. There was a sort of rivalry going on between the Samskrit and the Persian teachers. The Persian teacher was lenient. The boys used to talk among themselves that Persian was very easy and the Persian teacher very good and considerate to the students. The 'easiness' tempted me and one day I sat in the Persian class. The Samskrit teacher was grieved. He called me to his side and said: 'How can you forget that you are the son of a Vaishnava father? Won't you learn the language of your own religion? If you have any difficulty, why not come to me? I want to teach you students Samskrit to the best of my ability. As you proceed further, you will find in it things of absorbing interest. You should not lose heart. Come and sit again in the Samskrit class.'

My teacher's kindness

This kindness put me to shame. I could not disregard my teacher's affection. Today I cannot but think with gratitude of Krishnashankar Pandya. For if I had not acquired the little Samskrit that I learnt then, I should have found it difficult to take any interest in our sacred books. In fact I deeply regret that I was not able to acquire a more thorough knowledge of the language, because I have since realized that every Hindu boy and girl should possess sound Samskrit learning.

On Indian curricula

It is now my opinion that in all Indian curricula of higher education there should be a place for Hindi, Samskrit, Persian, Arabic and English, besides of course the vernacular. This big list need not frighten anyone. If our education were more systematic, and the boys free from the burden of having to learn their subjects through a foreign medium, I am sure learning all these languages would not be an irksome task, but a perfect pleasure. A scientific knowledge of one language makes a knowledge of other languages comparatively easy.

Indian languages

In reality, Hindi, Gujarati and Samskrit may be regarded as one language, and Persian and Arabic also as one. Though Persian belongs to the Aryan, and Arabic to the Semitic family of languages, there is a close relationship between Persian and Arabic, because both claim their full growth through the rise of Islam. Urdu I have not regarded as a distinct language, because it has adopted the Hindi grammar and its vocabulary is mainly Persian and Arabic, and he who would learn good Urdu must learn Persian and Arabic, as one who would learn good Gujarati, Hindi, Bengali, or Marathi must learn Samskrit.

Hindu marriage

Marriage among Hindus is no simple matter. The parents of the bride and the bridegroom often bring themselves to ruin over it. They waste their substance, they waste their time. Months are taken up over the preparations – in making clothes and ornaments and in preparing budgets for dinners. Each tries to outdo the other in the number and variety of courses to be prepared. Women, whether they have a voice or no, sing themselves hoarse, even get ill, and disturb the peace of their neighbours. These in their turn quietly put up with all the turmoil and bustle, all the dirt and filth, representing the remains of the feasts, because they know that a time will come when they also will be behaving in the same manner.

Passions of the flesh

I was devoted to my parents. But no less was I devoted
to the passions that flesh is heir to. I had yet to learn
that all happiness and pleasure should be sacrificed in
devoted service to my parents. And yet, as though by way
of punishment for my desire for pleasures, an incident
happened, which has ever since rankled in my mind and
which I will relate later. Nishkulanand sings: 'Renunciation
of objects, without the renunciation of desires, is short-lived,
however hard you may try'. Whenever I sing this song or
hear it sung, this bitter untoward incident, rushes to my
memory and fills me with shame.

A triple wedding planned

It would be better, thought my elders, to have all this bother
over at one and the same time. Less expense and greater
éclat. For money could be freely spent if it had only to be
spent once instead of thrice. My father and my uncle were
both old, and we were the last children they had to marry.
It is likely that they wanted to have the last best time of their
lives. In view of all these considerations, a triple wedding
was decided upon, and as I have said before, months were
taken up in preparation for it.

Carnal desire

It was only through these preparations that we got warning
of the coming event. I do not think it meant to me anything
more than the prospect of good clothes to wear, drum
beating, marriage processions, rich dinners and a strange

girl to play with. The carnal desire came later. I propose to draw a curtain over my shame, except for a few details worth recording. To these I shall come later. But even they have little to do with the central idea I have kept before me in writing this story.

Smearing our bodies

So my brother and I were both taken to Porbandar from Rajkot. There are some amusing details of the preliminaries to the final drama – e.g. smearing our bodies all over with turmeric paste – but I must omit them.

My father's accident

My father was a Diwan, but nevertheless a servant, and all the more so because he was in favour with the Thakore Saheb. The latter would not let him go until the last moment. And when he did so, he ordered for my father special stage coaches, reducing the journey by two days. But the fates had willed otherwise. Porbandar is 120 miles from Rajkot – a cart journey of five days. My father did the distance in three, but the coach toppled over in the third stage, and he sustained severe injuries. He arrived bandaged all over. Both his and our interest in the coming event was half destroyed, but the ceremony had to be gone through. For how could the marriage dates be changed? However, I forgot my grief over my father's injuries in the childish amusement of the wedding.

Marriage pamphlets

About the time of my marriage, little pamphlets costing a pice, or a pie (I now forget how much), used to be issued, in which conjugal love, thrift, child marriages, and other such subjects were discussed. I used to go through them cover to cover, and it was a habit with me to forget what I did not like, and to carry out in practice whatever I liked. Lifelong faithfulness to the wife, inculcated in these booklets as the duty of the husband, remained permanently imprinted on my heart. Furthermore, the passion for truth was innate in me, and to be false to her was therefore out of the question. And then there was very little chance of my being faithless at that tender age.

Problems of fidelity

But the lesson of faithfulness had also an untoward effect. 'If I should be pledged to be faithful to my wife, she also should be pledged to be faithful to me', I said to myself. The thought made me a jealous husband. Her duty was easily converted into my right to exact faithfulness from her, and if it had to be exacted, I should be watchfully tenacious of the right. I had absolutely no reason to suspect my wife's fidelity, but jealousy does not wait for reasons. I must need be for ever on the look-out regarding her movements, and therefore she could not go anywhere without my permission. This sowed the seeds of a bitter quarrel between us. The restraint was virtually a sort of imprisonment. And Kasturbai was not the girl to brook any such thing. She made it a point to go out whenever and wherever she liked. More restraint on my part resulted in more liberty being taken by her, and in my getting more and more cross. Refusal to speak to one another thus became the order of the day with us, married children. I think it was quite innocent of Kasturbai to have taken those liberties with my restrictions. How could a guileless girl brook any restraint on going to the temple or on going on visits to friends? If I had the right to impose restrictions on her, had not she also similar right? All this is clear to me today. But at that time I had to make good my authority as a husband!

Severity based on love

Let not the reader think, however, that ours was a life of unrelieved bitterness. For my severities were all based on love. I wanted to make my wife an ideal wife. My ambition was to make her live a pure life, learn what I learnt, and identify her life and thought with mine.

My wife Kasturbai

I do not know whether Kasturbai had any such ambition. She was illiterate. By nature she was simple, independent, persevering and, with me at least, reticent. She was not impatient of her ignorance and I do not recollect my studies having ever spurred her to go in for a similar adventure. I fancy, therefore, that my ambition was all one-sided. My passion was entirely centred on one woman, and I wanted it to be reciprocated. But even if there were no reciprocity, it could not be all unrelieved misery because there was active love on one side at least.

Passion for my wife

I must say I was passionately fond of her. Even at school I used to think of her, and the thought of nightfall and our subsequent meeting was ever haunting me. Separation was unbearable. I used to keep her awake till late in the night with my idle talk. If with this devouring passion there had not been in me a burning attachment to duty, I should either have fallen a prey to disease and premature death, or have sunk into a burdensome existence. But the appointed tasks had to be gone through every morning, and lying to anyone was out of the question. It was this last thing that saved me from many a pitfall.

Instructing my wife

I have already said that Kasturbai was illiterate. I was very anxious to teach her, but lustful love left me no time. For one thing the teaching had to be done against her will, and that too at night. I dared not meet her in the presence of the elders, much less talk to her. Kathiawad had then, and to a certain extent has even today, its own peculiar, useless and barbarous Purdah. Circumstances were thus unfavourable. I must therefore confess that most of my efforts to instruct Kasturbai in our youth were unsuccessful. And when I awoke from the sleep of lust, I had already launched forth into public life, which did not leave me much spare time. I failed likewise to instruct her through private tutors. As a result Kasturbai can now with difficulty write simple letters and understand simple Gujarati. I am sure that, had my love for her been absolutely untainted with lust, she would be a learned lady today; for I could than have conquered her dislike for studies. I know that nothing is impossible for pure love.

God saves the pure

I have mentioned one circumstance that more or less saved me from the disasters of lustful love. There is another worth noting. Numerous examples have convinced me that God ultimately saves him whose motive is pure. Along with the cruel custom of child marriages, Hindu society has another custom which to a certain extent diminishes the evils of the former. Parents do not allow young couples to stay long together. The child-wife spends more than half her time at her father's place. Such was the case with us. That is to say, during the first five years of our married life (from the age of 13 to 18), we could not have lived together longer than an aggregate period of three years. We would hardly have spent six months together, when there would be a call to my wife from her parents. Such calls were very unwelcome in those days, but they saved us both. At the age of eighteen I went to England, and this meant a long and healthy spell of separation. Even after my return from England we hardly stayed together longer than six months. For I had to run up and down between Rajkot and Bombay. Then came the call from South Africa, and that found me already fairly free from the carnal appetite.

Once receiving corporal punishment

My own recollection is that I had not any high regard for
my ability. I used to be astonished whenever I won prizes
and scholarships. But I very jealously guarded my character. The least little blemish drew tears from my eyes. When
I merited, or seemed to the teacher to merit, a rebuke, it
was unbearable for me. I remember having once received
corporal punishment. I did not so much mind the punishment as the fact that it was considered my dessert. I wept
piteously. That was when I was in the first or second
standard. There was another such incident during the
time when I was in the seventh standard. Dorabji Edulji
Gimi was the headmaster then. He was popular among
boys, as he was a disciplinarian, a man of method and a
good teacher. He had made gymnastics and cricket compulsory for boys of the upper standards. I disliked both. I
never took part in any exercise, cricket or football, before
they were made compulsory. My shyness was one of the
reasons for this aloofness, which I now see was wrong. I
then had the false notion that gymnastics had nothing to
do with education. Today I know that physical training
should have as much place in the curriculum as mental
training.

My friendships

Amongst my few friends at the high school I had, at
different times, two who might be called intimate. One of
these friendships did not last long, though I never forsook
my friend. He forsook me, because I made friends with the

other. This latter friendship I regard as a tragedy in my life. It lasted long. I formed it in spirit of a reformer.

My elder brother's friend

This companion was originally my elder brother's friend. They were classmates. I knew his weakness, but I regarded him as a faithful friend. My mother, my eldest brother, and my wife warned me that I was in bad company. I was too proud to heed my wife's warning. But I dared not go against the opinion of my mother and my eldest brother. Nevertheless I pleaded with them saying, 'I know he has the weaknesses you attribute to him, but you do not know his virtues. He cannot lead me astray, as my association with him is meant to reform him. For I am sure that if he reforms his ways, he will be a splendid man. I beg you not to be anxious on my account.' I do not think this satisfied them, but they accepted my explanation and let me go my way.

A miscalculation

I have seen since that I had calculated wrongly. A reformer cannot afford to have close intimacy with him whom he seeks to reform. True friendship is an identity of souls rarely to be found in this world. Only between like natures can friendship be altogether worthy and enduring. Friends react on one another. Hence in friendship there is very little scope for reform. I am of opinion that all exclusive intimacies are to be avoided; for man takes in vice far more readily than virtue. And he who would be friends with God must remain alone, or make the whole world his friend. I may be wrong, but my effort to cultivate an intimate friendship proved a failure.

Meat-eating teachers

A wave of 'reform' was sweeping over Rajkot at the time when I first came across this friend. He informed me that many of our teachers were secretly taking meat and wine. He also named many well-known people of Rajkot as belonging to the same company. There were also, I was told, some high-school boys among them.

Dangers of meat eating

I was surprised and pained. I asked my friend the reason and he explained it thus: 'We are a weak people because we do not eat meat. The English are able to rule over us, because they are meat-eaters. You know how hardy I am, and how great a runner too. It is because I am a meat-eater. Meat-eaters do not have boils or tumours, and even if they sometimes happen to have any, these heal quickly. Our teachers and other distinguished people who eat meat are no fools. They know its virtues. You should do likewise. There is nothing like trying. Try, and see what strength it gives.'

Further pleas regarding meat eating

All these pleas on behalf of meat eating were not advanced at a single sitting. They represent the substance of a long and elaborate argument which my friend was trying to impress upon me from time to time. My elder brother had already fallen. He therefore supported my friend's argument. I certainly looked feeble-bodied by the side of my brother and this friend. They were both hardier, physically stronger, and more daring. This friend's exploits cast a spell over me. He could run long distances and extraordinarily fast. He was an adept in high and long jumping. He could put up with any amount of corporal punishment. He would often display his exploits to me and, as one is always dazzled when he sees in others the qualities that he lacks himself, I was dazzled by this friend's exploits. This was followed by a strong desire to be like him. I could hardly jump or run. Why should not I also be as strong as he?

My cowardice

Moreover, I was a coward. I used to be haunted by the fear of thieves, ghosts and serpents. I did not dare to stir out of doors at night. Darkness was a terror to me. It was almost impossible for me to sleep in the dark, as I would imagine ghosts coming from one direction, thieves from another and serpents from a third. I could not therefore bear to sleep without a light in the room. How could I disclose my fears to my wife, no child, but already at the threshold of youth, sleeping by my side? I knew that she had more courage than I, and I felt ashamed of myself. She knew no fear of serpents and ghosts. She could go out anywhere in the dark. My friend knew all these weaknesses of mine. He would tell me that he could hold in his hand live serpents, could defy thieves and did not believe in ghosts. And all this was, of course, the result of eating meat.

A doggerel verse

A doggerel of the Gujarati poet Narmad was in vogue amongst us schoolboys, as follows:

Behold the mighty Englishman
He rules the Indian small,
Because being a meat-eater
He is five cubits tall.

Conversion against meat eating

All this had its due effect on me. I was beaten. It began to grow on me that meat-eating was good, that it would make me strong and daring, and that, if the whole county took to meat-eating, the English could be overcome.

My experiment

A day was thereupon fixed for beginning the experiment. It had to be conducted in secret. The Gandhis were Vaishnavas. My parents were particularly staunch Vaishnavas. They would regularly visit the Haveli. The family had even its own temples. Jainism was strong in Gujarat, and its influence was felt everywhere and on all occasions. The opposition to and abhorrence of meat-eating that existed in Gujarat among the Jains and Vaishnavas were to be seen nowhere else in India or outside in such strength. These were the traditions in which I was born and bred. And I was extremely devoted to my parents. I knew that the moment they came to know of my having eaten meat, they would be shocked to death. Moreover, my love of truth made me extra cautious. I cannot say that I did not know then that I should have to deceive my parents if I began eating meat. But my mind was bent on the 'reform'. It was not a question of pleasing the palate. I did not know that it had a particularly good relish. I wished to be strong and daring and wanted my countrymen also to be such, so that we might defeat the English and make India free. The word Swaraj I had not yet heard. But I knew what freedom meant. The frenzy of the 'reform' blinded me. And having ensured secrecy, I persuaded myself that mere hiding the deed from parents was no departure from truth.

So the day came. It is difficult fully to describe my condition. There were, on the one hand, the zeal for 'reform', and the novelty of making a momentous departure in life. There was, on the other, the shame of hiding like a thief to do this very thing. I cannot say which of the two swayed me more. We went in search of a lonely spot by the river, and there I saw, for the first time in my life – meat. There was baker's bread also. I relished neither. The goat's meat was as tough as leather. I simply could not eat it. I was sick and had to leave off eating. I had a very bad night afterwards. A horrible night-mare haunted me. Every time I dropped off to sleep it would seem as though a live goat were bleating inside me, and I would jump up full of remorse. But then I would remind myself that meat-eating was a duty and so become more cheerful.

My friend was not a man to give in easily. He now began to cook various delicacies with meat, and dress them neatly. And for dining, no longer was the secluded spot on the river chosen, but a State house, with its dining hall, and tables and chairs, about which my friend had made arrangements in collusion with the chief cook there.

My friend succeeds

This bait had its effect. I got over my dislike for bread, forswore my compassion for the goats, and became a relisher of meat-dishes, if not of meat itself. This went on for about a year. But not more than half a dozen meat-feasts were enjoyed in all; because the State house was not available every day, and there was the obvious difficulty about frequently preparing expensive savoury meat-dishes. I had no money to pay for this 'reform'. My friend had therefore always to find the wherewithal. I had no knowledge where he found it. But find it he did, because he was bent on turning me into a meat-eater. But even his means must have been limited, and hence these feasts had necessarily to be few and far between.

Surreptitious feasts

Whenever I had occasion to indulge in these surreptitious feasts, dinner at home was out of the question. My mother would naturally ask me to come and take my food and want to know the reason why I did not wish to eat. I would say to her, 'I have no appetite today; there is something wrong with my digestion.' It was not without compunction that I devised these pretexts. I knew I was lying, and lying to my mother. I also knew that, if my mother and father came to know of my having become a meat-eater, they would be deeply shocked. This knowledge was gnawing at my heart. Therefore I said to myself: 'Though it is essential to eat meat, and also essential to take up food 'reform' in the country, yet deceiving and lying to one's father and mother is worse than not eating meat. In their lifetime, therefore, meat-eating must be out of the question. When they are no more and I have found my freedom, I will eat meat openly, but until that moment arrives I will abstain from it.

The end of meat eating

This decision I communicated to my friend, and I have never since gone back to meat. My parents never knew that two of their sons had become meat-eaters.

I abjured meat out of the purity of my desire not to lie to my parents, but I did not abjure the company of my friend. My zeal for reforming him had proved disastrous for me, and all the time I was completely unconscious of the fact.

A visit to a brothel

The same company would have led me into faithlessness to my wife. But I was saved by the skin of my teeth. My friend once took me to a brothel. He sent me in with the necessary instructions. It was all prearranged. The bill had already been paid. I went into the jaws of sin, but God in His infinite mercy protected me against myself. I was almost struck blind and dumb in this den of vice. I sat near the woman on her bed, but I was tongue-tied. She naturally lost patience with me, and showed me the door, with abuses and insults. I then felt as though my manhood had been injured, and wished to sink into the ground for shame. But I have ever since given thanks to God for having saved me. I can recall four more similar incidents in my life, and in most of them my good fortune, rather than any effort on my part, saved me. From a strictly ethical point of view, all these occasions must be regarded as moral lapses; for the carnal desire was there, and it was as good as the act. But from the ordinary point of view, a man who is saved from physically committing sin is regarded as saved. And I was saved only in that sense. There are some actions from which an escape is a godsend both for the man who escapes and for those about him. Man, as soon as he gets back his consciousness of right, is thankful to the Divine mercy for the escape. As we know that a man often succumbs to temptation, however much he say resist it, we also know that Providence often intercedes and saves him in spite of himself. How all this happens – how far a man is free and how far a creature of circumstances – how far free-will comes into play and where fate enters on the scene – all this is a mystery and will remain a mystery.

But to go on with the story. Even this was far from opening my eyes to the viciousness of my friend's company. I therefore had many more bitter draughts in store for me, until my eyes were actually opened by an ocular demonstration of some of his lapses quite unexpected by me.

Relationship with my wife

One thing, however, I must mention now, as it pertains to the same period. One of the reasons of my differences with my wife was undoubtedly the company of this friend. I was both a devoted and a jealous husband, and this friend fanned the flame of my suspicions about my wife. I never could doubt his veracity. And I have never forgiven myself the violence of which I have been guilty in often having pained my wife by acting on his information. Perhaps only a Hindu wife would tolerate these hardships, and that is why I have regarded woman as an incarnation of tolerance. A servant wrongly suspected may throw up his job, a son in the same case may leave his father's roof, and a friend may put an end to the friendship. A wife, if she suspects her husband, will keep quiet, but if her husband suspects her, she is ruined. Where is she to go? A Hindu wife may not seek divorce in a law-court. Law has no remedy for her. And I can never forget or forgive myself for a having driven my wife to that desperation.

Ahisma and Brahmacharya

The canker of suspicion was rooted out only when I understood Ahimsa[1] in all its bearings. I saw then the glory of Brahmacharya[2] and realized that the wife is not the husband's bondslave, but his companion and his helpmate, and an equal partner in all his joys and sorrows – as free as the husband to choose her own path. Whenever I think of those dark days of doubts and suspicions, I am filled with loathing of my folly and my lustful cruelty, and I deplore my blind devotion to a friend.

[1.] 'Ahimsa' means literally not-hurting, non-violence.

[2.] 'Brahmacharya' means literally conduct that leads one to God. Its technical meaning is self-restraint, particularly mastery over the sexual organ.

I have still to relate some of my failings during this meat-eating period and also previous to it, which date from before my marriage or soon after.

Tobacco smoking

A relative and I became fond of smoking. Not that we saw any good in smoking, or were enamoured of the smell of a cigarette. We simply imagined a sort of pleasure in emitting clouds of smoke from our mouths. My uncle had the habit, and when we saw him smoking, we thought we should copy his example. But we had no money. So we began to pilfer stumps of cigarettes thrown away by my uncle.

Stealing

The stumps, however, were not always available, and could not emit much smoke either. So we began to steal coppers from the servant's pocket money in order to purchase Indian cigarettes. But the question was where to keep them. We could not of course smoke in the presence of elders. We managed somehow for a few weeks on these stolen coppers. In the meantime we heard that the stalks of a certain plant were porous and could be smoked like cigarettes. We got them and began this kind of smoking. But we were far from being satisfied with such things as these. Our want of independence began to smart. It was unbearable that we should be unable to do anything without the elders' permission. At last, in sheer disgust, we decided to commit suicide!

Contemplation of suicide

But how were we to do it? From where were we to get the poison? We heard that Dhatura seeds were an effective poison. Off we went to the jungle in search of these seeds, and got them. Evening was thought to be the auspicious hour. We went to Kedarji Mandir, put ghee in the temple-lamp, had the darshan and then looked for a lonely corner. But our courage failed us. Supposing we were not instantly killed? And what was the good of killing ourselves? Why not rather put up with the lack of independence? But we swallowed two or three seeds nevertheless. We dared not take more. Both of us fought shy of death, and decided to go to Ramji Mandir to compose ourselves, and to dismiss the thought of suicide.

I realized that it was not as easy to commit suicide as to contemplate it. And since then, whenever I have heard of someone threatening to commit suicide, it has had little or on effect on me. The thought of suicide ultimately resulted in both of us bidding good-bye to the habit of smoking stumps of cigarettes and of stealing the servant's coppers for the purpose of smoking.

The end of smoking

Ever since I have been grown up, I have never desired to smoke and have always regarded the habit of smoking as barbarous, dirty and harmful. I have never understood why there is such a rage for smoking throughout the world. I cannot bear to travel in a compartment full of people smoking. I become choked.

More theft

But much more serious than this theft was the one I was guilty of a little later. I pilfered the coppers when I was twelve or thirteen, possibly less. The other theft was committed when I was fifteen. In this case I stole a bit of gold out of my meat-eating brother's armlet. This brother had run into a debt of about twenty-five rupees. He had on his arm an armlet of solid gold. It was not difficult to clip a bit out of it.

Well, it was done, and the debt cleared. But this became more than I could bear. I resolved never to steal again. I also made up my mind to confess it to my father. But I did not dare to speak. Not that I was afraid of my father beating me. No I do not recall his ever having beaten any of us. I was afraid of the pain that I should cause him. But I felt that the risk should be taken; that there could not be a cleansing without a confession.

My confession

I decided at last to write out the confession, to submit it to my father, and ask his forgiveness. I wrote it on a slip of paper and handed it to him myself. In this note not only did I confess my guilt, but I asked adequate punishment for it, and closed with a request to him not to punish himself for my offence. I also pledged myself never to steal in future.

I was trembling as I handed the confession to my father. He was then suffering from a fistula and was confined to bed. His bed was a plain wooden plank. I handed him the note and sat opposite the plank.

He read it through, and pearl-drops trickled down his

cheeks, wetting the paper. For a moment he closed his eyes in thought and then tore up the note. He had sat up to read it. He again lay down. I also cried. I could see my father's agony. If I were a painter I could draw a picture of the whole scene today. It is still so vivid in my mind.

My sins are cleansed

Those pearl-drops of love cleansed my heart, and washed my sin away. Only he who has experienced such love can know what it is. As the hymn says:

Only he
Who is smitten with the arrows of love,
Knows its power.

The power of Ahisma

This was, for me, an object-lesson in Ahimsa. Then I could read in it nothing more than a father's love, but today I know that it was pure Ahimsa. When such Ahimsa becomes all-embracing, it transforms everything it touches. There is no limit to its power. This sort of sublime forgiveness was not natural to my father. I had thought that he would be angry, say hard things, and strike his forehead. But he was so wonderfully peaceful, and I believe this was due to my clean confession. A clean confession, combined with a promise never to commit the sin again, when offered before one who has the right to receive it, is the purest type of repentance. I know that my confession made my father feel absolutely safe about me, and increased his affection for me beyond measure.

First glimpses of religion

From my sixth or seventh year up to my sixteenth I was at school, being taught all sorts of things except religion. I may say that I failed to get from the teachers what they could have given me without any effort on their part. And yet I kept on picking up things here and there from my surroundings. The term 'religion' I am using in its broadest sense, meaning thereby Self-realization or Knowledge of Self.

Ramanama

But what I failed to get there I obtained from my nurse, an old servant of the family, whose affection for me I still recall. I have said before that there was in me a fear of ghosts and spirits. Rambha, for that was her name, suggested, as a remedy for this fear, the repetition of Ramanama. I had more faith in her than in her remedy, and so at a tender age I began repeating Ramanama to cure my fear of ghosts and spirits. This was of course short-lived, but the good seed sown in childhood was not sown in vain. I think it is due to the seed sown by that good woman Rambha that today Ramanama is an infallible remedy for me.

What, however, left a deep impression on me was the reading of the Ramayana before my father. During part of his illness my father was in Porbandar. There every evening he used to listen to the Ramayana. The reader was a great devotee of Rama. That laid the foundation of my deep devotion to the Ramayana. Today I regard the Ramayana of Tulasidas as the greatest book in all devotional literature.

Morality

But one thing took deep root in me – the conviction that morality is the basis of things, and that truth is the substance of all morality. Truth became my sole objective. It began to grow in magnitude every day, and my definition of it also has been ever widening.

A Gujarati didactic stanza likewise gripped my mind and heart. Its precept – return good for evil – became my guiding principle. It became such a passion with me that I began numerous experiments in it. Here are those (for me) wonderful lines:

> For a bowl of water give a goodly meal:
> For a kindly greeting bow thou down with zeal:
> For a simple penny pay thou back with gold:
> If thy life be rescued, life do not withhold.
> Thus the words and actions of the wise regard;
> Every little service tenfold they reward.
> But the truly noble know all men as one,
> And return with gladness good for evil done.

PREPARATION FOR ENGLAND

I passed the matriculation examination in 1887. My elders wanted me to pursue my studies at college after the matriculation. I decided to join the Samaldas College. I went, but found myself entirely at sea. Everything was difficult. I could not follow, let alone taking interest in, the professors' lectures. It was no fault of theirs. The professors in that College were regarded as first rate. But I was so raw. At the end of the first term, I returned home.

We had, in Mavji Dave, who was a shrewd and learned Brahman an old friend and adviser of the family. He had kept up his connection with the family even after my father's death. He happened to visit us during my vacation. In conversation with my mother and elder brother, he inquired about my studies. Learning that I was at Samaldas College, he said: 'The times are changed. I would far rather that you sent him to England. My son Kevalram says it is very easy to become a barrister. In three years' time he will return. Hturned to me with complete assurance, and asked: 'Would you not rather go to England than study here?' Nothing could have been more welcome to me. I was fighting shy of my difficult studies. So I jumped at the proposal and said that the sooner I was sent the better. It was no easy business to pass examinations quickly. He said "Father intended you for the bar.' It is the wisest thing therefore to become a barrister.' Turning to my mother he said: 'Now, I must leave. Pray ponder over what I have said. When I come here next I shall expect to hear of preparations for England. Be sure to let me know if I can assist in any way.'

My uncle's permission

I went to see my uncle, and told him everything. He thought it over and said " I will not stand in your way. It is your mother's permission which really matters. If she permits you, then godspeed! Tell her I will not interfere. You will go with my blessings.'

My mother's consent

My mother, however, was still unwilling. She had begun making minute inquiries. Someone had told her that young men got lost in England. Someone else had said that they took to meat; and yet another that they could not live there without liquor. 'How about all this?' she asked me. I said: 'Will you not trust me? I shall not lie to you. I swear that I shall not touch any of those things. 'I can trust you,' she said. The high school had a send-off in my honour. I sailed from Bombay.

In London at last

I was very uneasy even in the new rooms. I would continually think of my home and country. My mother's love always haunted me. At night the tears would stream down my cheeks, and home memories of all sorts made sleep out of the question. It was impossible to share my misery with anyone. And even if I could have done so, where was the use? I knew of nothing that would soothe me. Everything was strange – the people, their ways, and even their dwellings. I was a complete novice in the matter of English etiquette and continually had to be on my guard. There was the additional inconvenience of the vegetarian vow. Even the dishes that I could eat were tasteless and insipid. I thus found myself between Scylla and Charybdis. England I could not bear, but to return to India was not to be thought of. Now that I had come, I must finish the three years, said the inner voice.

Acquaintance with religion: Theosophy

Towards the end of my second year in England I came across two Theosophists, brothers, and both unmarried. They talked to me about the Gita. They were reading Sir Edwin Arnold's translation – *The Song Celestial* – and they invited me to read the original with them. I felt ashamed, as I had read the divine poem neither in Samskrit nor in Gujarati. I was constrained to tell them that I had not read the Gita, but that I would gladly read it with them, and that though my knowledge of Samskrit was meagre, still I hoped to be able to understand the original to the extent of telling where the translation failed to bring out the meaning. I began reading the Gita with them. The verses in the second chapter

> If one
> Ponders on objects of the sense, there springs
> Attraction; from attraction grows desire,
> Desire flames to fierce passion, passion breeds
> Recklessness; then the memory–all betrayed–
> Lets noble purpose go, and saps the mind,
> Till purpose, mind, and man are all undone

made a deep impression on my mind, and they still ring in

my ears. The book struck me as one of priceless worth. The impression has ever since been growing on me with the result that I regard it today as the book par excellence for the knowledge of Truth. It has afforded me invaluable help in my moments of gloom. I have read almost all the English translations of it, and I regard Sir Edwin Arnold's as the best. He has been faithful to the text, and yet it does not read like a translation. Though I read the Gita with these friends, I cannot pretend to have studied it then. It was only after some years that it became a book of daily reading.

The brothers also recommended *The Light of Asia* by Sir Edwin Arnold, whom I knew till then as the author only of *The Song Celestial*, and I read it with even greater interest than I did the Bhagavadgita. Once I had begun it I could not leave off. They also took me on one occasion to the Blavatsky Lodge and introduced me to Madame Blavatsky and Mrs. Besant. The latter had just then joined the Theosophical Society, and I was following with great interest the controversy about her conversion. The friends advised me to join the Society, but I politely declined saying, 'With my meagre knowledge of my own religion I do not want to belong to any religious body.' I recall having read, at the brothers' instance, Madame Blavatsky's *Key to Theosophy*. This book stimulated in me the desire to read books on Hinduism, and disabused me of the notion fostered by the missionaries that Hinduism was rife with superstition.

I meet a good Christian

About the same time I met a good Christian from Manchester in a vegetarian boarding house. He talked to me about Christianity. I narrated to him my Rajkot recollections. He was pained to hear them. He said, 'I am a vegetarian. I do not drink. Many Christians are meat-eaters and drink, no doubt; but neither meat-eating nor drinking is enjoined by Scripture. Do please read the Bible.' I accepted his advice, and he got me a copy. I have a faint recollection that he himself used to sell copies of the Bible, and I purchased from him an edition containing maps, concordance, and other aids. I began reading it, but I could not possibly read through the Old Testament. I read the book of Genesis, and the chapters that followed invariably sent me to sleep. But just for the sake of being able to say that I had read it, I plodded through the other books with much difficulty and without the least interest or understanding. I disliked reading the book of Numbers.

But the New Testament produced a different impression, especially the Sermon on the Mount which went straight to my heart. I compared it with the Gita. The verses, 'But I say unto you, that ye resist not evil: but whosoever shall smite thee on thy right cheek, turn to him the other also. And if any man take away thy coat let him have thy cloke too,' delighted me beyond measure and put me in mind of Shamal Bhatt's 'For a bowl of water, give a goodly meal' etc. My young mind tried to unify the teaching of the Gita, the Light of Asia and the Sermon on the Mount. That renunciation was the highest form of religion appealed to me greatly.

This reading whetted my appetite for studying the lives of other religious teachers. A friend recommended Carlyle's *Heroes and Hero-Worship*. I read the chapter on the Hero as a prophet and learnt of the Prophet's greatness and bravery and austere living.

Beyond this acquaintance with religion I could not go at the moment, as reading for the examination left me scarcely any time for outside subjects. But I took mental note of the fact that I should read more religious books and acquaint myself with all the principal religions.

Atheism

And how could I help knowing something of atheism too? Every Indian knew Bradlaugh's name and his so-called atheism. I read some book about it, the name of which I forget. It had no effect on me, for I had already crossed the Sahara of atheism. Mrs. Besant, who was then very much in the limelight, had turned to theism from atheism, and that fact also strengthened my aversion to atheism. I had read her book How I became a Theosophist. It was about this time that Bradlaugh died. He was buried in the Working Cemetery. I attended the funeral, as I believe every Indian residing in London did. A few clergymen also were present to do him the last honours. On our way back from the funeral we had to wait at the station for our train. A champion atheist from the crowd heckled one of these clergymen. 'Well sir, you believe in the existence of God?'

'I do,' said the good man in a low tone. 'You also agree that the circumference of the Earth is 28,000 miles, don't you?' said the atheist with a smile of self-assurance. 'Indeed.'

'Pray tell me then the size of your God and where he may be?'

'Well, if we but knew, He resides in the hearts of us both.'

'Now, now, don't take me to be a child,' said the champion with a triumphant look at us.

The clergyman assumed a humble silence.

Being called to the Bar

There were two conditions which had to be fulfilled before a student was formally called to the bar: 'keeping terms,' twelve terms equivalent to about three years; and passing examinations. 'Keeping terms' meant eating one's terms, i.e., attending at least six out of about twenty-four dinners in a term. Eating did not mean actually partaking of the dinner, it meant reporting oneself at the fixed hours and remaining present throughout the dinner. Usually, of course, every one ate and drank the good commons and choice wines provided. A dinner cost from two and six to three and six, that is from two to three rupees. This was considered moderate, inasmuch as one had to pay that same amount for wines alone if one dined at a hotel. To us in India it is a matter for surprise, if we are not 'civilized', that the cost of drink should exceed the cost of food. The first revelation gave me a great shock, and I wondered how people had the heart to throw away so much money on drink. Later I came to understand. I often ate nothing at these dinners, for the things that I might eat were only bread, boiled potato and cabbage. In the beginning I did not eat these, as I did not like them; and later, when I began to relish them, I also gained the courage to ask for other dishes.

The dinner provided for the benchers used to be better than that for the students. A Parsi student, who was also a vegetarian, and I applied, in the interests of vegetarianism, for the vegetarian courses which were served to the benchers. The application was granted, and we began to get fruits and other vegetables from the benchers' table. I could not see then, nor have I seen since, how these dinners qualified the students better for the bar. There was once a time when only a few students used to attend these dinners and thus there were opportunities for talks between them and the benchers, and speeches were also made. These occasions helped to give them knowledge of the world with a sort of polish and refinement, and also improved their power of speaking. No such thing was possible in my time, as the benchers had a table all to themselves. The institution had gradually lost all its meaning, but conservative England retained it nevertheless.

The curriculum

The curriculum of study was easy, barristers being humorously known as 'dinner barristers'. Everyone knew that the examinations had practically no value. In my time there were two, one in Roman Law and the other in Common Law. There were regular text-books prescribed for these examinations which could be taken in compartments, but scarcely any one read them. I have known many to pass the Roman Law examination by scrambling through notes on Roman Law in a couple of weeks, and the Common Law examination by reading notes on the subject in two or three months. Question papers were easy and examiners were generous. The percentage of passes in the Roman Law examination used to be 95 to 99 and of those in the final examination 75 or even more. There was thus little fear of being picked, and examinations were held not once but four times in the year. They could not be felt as a difficulty.

But I succeeded in turning them into one. I felt that I should read all the text-books. It was a fraud, I thought, not to read these books. I invested much money in them. I decided to read Roman Law in Latin. The Latin which I had acquired in the London Matriculation stood me in good stead. And all this reading was not without its value later on in South Africa, where Roman Dutch is the common law. The reading of Justinian, therefore, helped me a great deal in understanding the South African law.

In the meantime while in India attempting to practice Law, a Meman firm from Porbandar wrote to my brother making the following offer: 'We have business in South Africa. Ours is a big firm, and we have a big case there in the Court, our claim being £40,000. It has been going on for a long time. We have engaged the services of the best vakils and barristers. If you sent your brother there, he would be useful to us and also to himself. He would be able to instruct our counsel better than ourselves. And he would have the advantage of seeing a new part of the world, and of making new acquaintances.'

My brother discussed the proposition with me. I could

not clearly make out whether I had simply to instruct the counsel or to appear in court. But I was tempted.

My brother introduced me to the late Sheth Abdul Karim Jhaveri a partner of Dada Abdulla & Co., the firm in question. 'It won't be a difficult job,' the Sheth assured me. 'We have big Europeans as our friends, whose acquaintance you will make. You can be useful to us in our shop. Much of our correspondence is in English and you can help us with that too. You will, of course, be our guest and hence will have no expense whatever.' 'How long do you require my services?' I asked. 'And what will be the payment?'

'Not more than a year. We will pay you a first class return fare and a sum of £105, all found.'

This was hardly going there as a barrister. It was going as a servant of the firm. But I wanted somehow to leave India. There was also the tempting opportunity of seeing a new country, and of having new experience. Also I could send £105 to my brother and help in the expenses of the household. I closed with the offer without any haggling, and got ready to go to South Africa.

LEAVING FOR SOUTH AFRICA

When starting for South Africa I did not feel the wrench of separation which I had experienced when leaving for England. My mother was now no more. I had gained some knowledge of the world and of travel abroad, and going from Rajkot to Bombay was no unusual affair.

In Pretoria

My first step was to call a meeting of all the Indians in Pretoria and to present to them a picture of their condition in the Transvaal. The meeting was held at the house of Sheth Haji Muhammad Haji Joosab, to whom I had a letter of introduction. It was principally attended by Meman merchants, though there was a sprinkling of Hindus as well. The Hindu population in Pretoria was, as a matter of fact, very small.

My speech at this meeting may be said to have been the first public speech in my life. I went fairly prepared with my subject, which was about observing truthfulness in business. I had always heard the merchants say that truth was not possible in business. I did not think so then, nor do I now. Even today there are merchant friends who contend that truth is inconsistent with business. Business, they say, is a very practical affair, and truth a matter of religion; and they argue that practical affairs are one thing, while religion is quite another. Pure truth, they hold, is out of the question in business, one can speak it only so far as is suitable. I strongly contested the position in my speech and awakened the merchants to a sense of their duty, which was two-fold. Their responsibility to be truthful was all the greater in a foreign land, because the conduct of a few Indians was the measure of that of the millions of their fellow-countrymen.

God laid the foundations of my life in South Africa and sowed the seed of the fight for national self-respect.

This time I only felt the pang of parting with my wife. Another baby had been born to us since my return from England. Our love could not yet be called free from lust, but it was getting gradually purer. Since my return from Europe, we had lived very little together; and as I had now become her teacher, however indifferent, and helped her to make certain reforms, we both felt the necessity of being more together, if only to continue the reforms. But the attraction of South Africa rendered the separation bearable. 'We are bound to meet again in a year,' I said to her, by way of consolation, and left Rajkot for Bombay.

The Common Law

It took me nine months of fairly hard labour to read through the Common Law of England. For Broom's Common Law, a big but interesting volume, took up a good deal of time. Snell's Equity was full of interest, but a bit hard to understand. White and Tudor's Leading Cases, from which certain cases were prescribed, was full of interest and instruction. I read also with interest Williams' and Edward's Real Property, and Goodeve's Personal Property. Williams' book read like a novel. The one book I remember to have read, on my return to India, with the same unflagging interest, was Mayne's

Hindu Law. But it is out of place to talk here of Indian law books. I passed my examinations, was called to the bar on the 10th of June 1891, and enrolled in the High Court on the 11th. On the 12th I sailed for home.

My profession

My profession progressed satisfactorily, but that was far from satisfying me. The question of further simplifying my life and of doing some concrete act of service to my fellowmen had been constantly agitating me, when a leper came to my door. I had not the heart to dismiss him with a meal. So I offered him shelter, dressed his wounds, and began to look after him. But I could not go on like that indefinitely. I could not afford, I lacked the will, to keep him always with me. So I sent him to the government hospital for indentured labourers.

After three years

By now I had been three years in South Africa. I had got to know the people and they had got to know me. In 1896 I asked permission to go home for six months, for I saw that I was in for a long stay there. I had established a fairly good practice, and could see that people felt the need of my presence. So I made up my mind to go home, fetch my wife and children, and then return and settle out there. I also saw that, if I went home, I might be able to do there some public work by educating public opinion and creating more interest in the Indians of South Africa. The £3 tax was an open sore. There could be no peace until it was abolished.

IN INDIA

I went straight to Rajkot without halting at Bombay and began to make preparations for writing a pamphlet on the situation in South Africa. The writing and publication of the pamphlet took about a month. It had a green cover and came to be known afterwards as the Green Pamphlet. In it I drew a purposely subdued picture of the conditions of Indians in South Africa. The language I used was more moderate than that of the two pamphlets which I have referred to before, as I knew that things heard of from a distance appear bigger than they are.

Ten thousand copies were printed and sent to all the papers and leaders of every party in India. The Pioneer was the first to notice it editorially. A summary of the article was cabled by Reuter to England, and a summary of that summary was cabled to Natal by Reuter's London office. This cable was not longer than three lines in print. It was a miniature, but exaggerated, edition of the picture I had drawn of the treatment accorded to the Indians in Natal, and it was not in my words. We shall see later on the effect this had in Natal. In the meanwhile every paper of note commented at length on the question.

The Congress

After reaching India I spent some time in going about the country. It was the year 1901 when the Congress met at Calcutta under the Presidentship of Mr. (later Sir) Dinshaw Wacha. And I of course attended it. It was my first experience of the Congress.

My resolution

As soon as it was time for my resolution, Mr. Wacha called out my name. I stood up. My head was reeling. I read the resolution somehow. Someone had printed and distributed amongst the delegates copies of a poem he had written in praise of foreign emigration. I read the poem and referred to the grievances of the settlers in South Africa. Just at this moment Mr. Wacha rang the bell. I was sure I had not yet spoken for five minutes. I did not know that the bell was rung in order to warn me to finish in two minutes more. I had heard others speak for half an hour or three quarters of an hour, and yet no bell was rung for them. I felt hurt and sat down as soon as the bell was rung. But my childlike intellect thought then that the poem contained an answer to Sir Pherozeshah.[1] There was no question about the passing of the re solution. In those days there was hardly any difference between visitors and delegates. Everyone raised his hand and all resolutions passed unanimously. My resolution also fared in this wise and so lost all its importance for me. And yet the very fact that it was passed by the Congress was enough to delight my heart. The knowledge that the imprimatur of the Congress meant that of the whole country was enough to delight anyone.

The founding of the Ashram

The Satyagraha Ashram was founded on the 25th of May, 1915. Shraddhanandji wanted me to settle in Hardvar. Some of my Calcutta friends recommended Vaidyanathadham. Others strongly urged me to choose Rajkot. But when I happened to pass through Ahmedabad, many friends pressed me to settle down there, and they volunteered to find the expenses of the Ashram, as well as a house for us to live in. The first thing we had to settle was the name of the Ashram. I consulted friends. Amongst the names suggested were 'Sevashram' (the abode of service), 'Tapovan' (the abode of austerities) etc. I liked the name 'Sevashram' but for the absence of emphasis on the method of service. 'Tapovan' seemed to be a pretentious title, because though tapas was dear to us we would not presume to be tapasvins (men of austerity). Our creed was devotion to truth, and our business was the search for and insistence on truth. I wanted to acquaint India with the method I had tried in South Africa, and I desired to test in India the extent to which its application might be possible. So my companions and I selected the name 'Satyagraha Ashram', as conveying both our goal and our method of service.

The conduct of the Ashram

For the conduct of the Ashram a code of rules and observances was necessary. A draft was therefore prepared, and friends were invited to express their opinions on it. Amongst the many opinions that were received, that of Sir Gurudas Banerji is still in my memory. He liked the rules, but suggested that humility should be added as one of the observances, as he believed that the younger generation sadly lacked humility. Though I noticed this fault, I feared humility would cease to be humility the moment it became a matter of vow. The true connotation of humility is self-effacement. Self-effacement is moksha (salvation), and whilst it cannot, by itself, be an observance, there may be other observances necessary for its attainment. If the acts of an aspirant after moksha or a servant have no humility or selflessness about them, there is no longing for moksha or service. Service without humility is selfishness and egotism.

My public life

My life from this point onward has been so public that there is hardly anything about it that people do not know. Moreover, since 1921 I have worked in such close association with the Congress leaders that I can hardly describe any episode in my life since then without referring to my relations with them. For though Shraddhanandji, the Deshabandhu, Hakim Saheb and Lalaji are no more with us today, we have the good luck to have a host of other veteran Congress leaders still living and working in our midst. The history of the Congress, since the great changes in it that I have described above, is still in the making. And my principal experiments during the past seven years have all been made through the Congress. A reference to my relations with the leaders would therefore be unavoidable, if I set about describing my experiments further. And this I may not do, at any rate for the present, if only from a sense of propriety. Lastly, my conclusions from my current experiments can hardly as yet be regarded as decisive. It therefore seems to me to be my plain duty to close this narrative here. In fact my pen instinctively refuses to proceed further.

Taking leave

It is not without a wrench that I have to take leave of the reader. I set a high value on my experiments. I do not know whether I have been able to do justice to them. I can only say that I have spared no pains to give a faithful narrative. To describe truth, as it has appeared to me, and in the exact manner in which I have arrived at it, has been my ceaseless effort. The exercise has given me ineffable mental peace, because, it has been my fond hope that it might bring faith in Truth and Ahimsa to waverers.

No other God but Truth

My uniform experience has convinced me that there is no other God than Truth. And if every page of these chapters does not proclaim to the reader that the only means for the realization of Truth is Ahimsa, I shall deem all my labour in writing these chapters to have been in vain. And, even though my efforts in this behalf may prove fruitless, let the readers know that the vehicle, not the great principle, is at fault. After all, however sincere my strivings after Ahimsa may have been, they have still been imperfect and inadequate. The little fleeting glimpses, therefore, that I have been able to have of Truth can hardly convey an idea of the indescribable lustre of Truth, a million times more intense than that of the sun we daily see with our eyes. In fact what I have caught is only the faintest glimmer of that mighty effulgence. But this much I can say with assurance, as a result of all my experiments, that a perfect vision of Truth can only follow a complete realization of Ahimsa.

To see the universal and all-pervading Spirit of Truth face to face one must be able to love the meanest of creation as oneself. And a man who aspires after that cannot afford to keep out of any field of life. That is why my devotion to Truth has drawn me into the field of politics; and I can say without the slightest hesitation, and yet in all humility, that those who say that religion has nothing to do with politics do not know what religion means.

Need for self-purification

Identification with everything that lives is impossible without self-purification; without self-purification the observance of the law of Ahimsa must remain an empty dream; God can never be realized by one who is not pure of heart. Self-purification therefore must mean purification in all the walks of life. And purification being highly infectious, purification of oneself necessarily leads to the purification of one's surroundings.

But the path of self-purification is hard and steep. To attain to perfect purity one has to become absolutely passion-free in thought, speech and action; to rise above the opposing currents of love and hatred, attachment and repulsion. I know that I have not in me as yet that triple purity, in spite of constant ceaseless striving for it. That is why the world's praise fails to move me, indeed it very often stings me. To conquer the subtle passions seems to me to be harder far than the physical conquest of the world by the force of arms. Ever since my return to India I have had experience of the dormant passions lying hidden within me. The knowledge of them has made me feel humiliated though not defeated. The experiences and experiments have sustained me and given me great joy. But I know that I have still before me a difficult path to traverse. I must reduce myself to zero. So long as a man does not of his own free will put himself last among his fellow creatures, there is no salvation for him. Ahimsa is the farthest limit of humility.

Farewell to the reader

In bidding farewell to the reader, for the time being at any rate, I ask him to join with me in prayer to the God of Truth that He may grant me the boon of Ahimsa in mind, word and deed.

EDITOR'S NOTE

Gandhi returned to his native country and commenced a practice in Bombay without a great deal of success. But then came a great opportunity: an Indian Company with interests in South Africa engaged him as their legal adviser with an office in Durban. Arriving in South Africa, the young Gandhi was shocked to find himself treated and regarded as a member of an inferior race. He was appalled at the widespread denial of both civil liberties and political rights to both Indian immigrants and the resident Indian community. He then decided to throw himself determinedly into the struggle for equal rights for Indians resident in South Africa.

As a consequence of his struggle and efforts to obtain these rights, he suffered many terms of imprisonment by the harshly prejudiced South African government and suffered both personal attacks and considerable humiliation. He stayed in South Africa for twenty years and decided to teach a policy of passive resistance and non-cooperation with the South African authorities. These ideas came from the Russian writer Leo Tolstoy, who was a great influence on the young Mohandas. Also while in India he came across a copy of Sir Edwin Arnold's poetic translation of the *Bhagavad Gita*, which electrified him, as the great spiritual heritage of his native country dawned upon his young mind. Later he acknowledged his debt to the teachings of Jesus Christ and the American civil rights activist of the time, the writer Henry David Thoreau, who had written a seminal essay on civil disobedience. He later coined the term 'Satyagraha', which meant 'truth and firmness' in Sanskrit, to typify his mission.

In order to appear patriotic, he enlisted in the British Army's Ambulance Corps during the Boer War. After the war he returned to his political campaign and commenced a cooperative farm near Durban. By 1914 he had gained some success when the South African government decided to legally recognize Indian marriages and abolition of their poll tax. At this juncture he decided to return to India.

On his return to his homeland, beloved India, Gandhi toured the country to survey the country's condition. He soon determined the necessity of liberating his country from the four hundred years of British Rule, which had plundered the country's manpower and resources. The British responded by imposing emergency powers after Gandhi encouraged civil disobedience as the means for realizing Home Rule. Overreaction by the British led to a massacre at Amritsar in 1920 that forced the Mahatma to adopt a policy of non-cooperation, and civil society went through a crisis. There was widespread poverty throughout the country, and to remedy this he adopted a policy of reviving cottage industry, adopting the spinning wheel as a symbol of the return to simple village life and the renewal of native industries.

He quickly became the emblematic hero of the movement towards a free India. He set an example to the nation by living a strict, spiritually ascetic life in the best traditions of Hinduism. His charismatic influence on the nation was so great that the British authorities were careful not to interfere with him. But in 1921, the Indian National Congress, which was the vanguard of the independence movement, gave him complete leadership and authority. More civil disobedience broke out, and in desperation the British imprisoned him from 1922 until 1924. After his release, he devoted himself to propagating communal unity. But in 1930 he called on the population to refuse to pay taxes, particularly the tax on salt. After a march that ended in violence, he was again arrested and was not released until 1931, when he halted his campaign after the British made concessions. However, in 1932 he resumed his campaign and was arrested twice. He went on hunger strikes, which were successful because the British knew that if he died there could well be a revolution.

A crucial year was 1934, when he decided to resign from politics and hand over the leadership of the Congress Party to the experienced and trusted politician Jawaharlal Nehru, while he travelled through India advocating non-violence and demanding the total eradication of the despicable custom of 'untouchability'. In 1935, the British decided to grant limited Home Rule to avoid further trouble and disturbance. In 1939, however, Gandhi returned to active politics because of the threatened federation of Autocratic Indian Principalities with the rest of India. He again fasted to enforce rajahs to relinquish their dictatorial rule.

When the Second World War broke out in 1939, the party under his influence decided not to support British war aims unless India was granted complete and immediate independence. The British adamantly refused to do this.

He was interned in 1942, but was released in 1944 when his health began to fail.

By 1944, his great struggle for independence was in its final stages, and the British Government agreed to complete Home Rule on the condition that the Muslim League and the Congress Party should resolve their differences. Gandhi was initially opposed to Partition, but eventually was forced to agree for the sake of internal peace. As a consequence, India and Pakistan became separate states. Riots followed Partition, and the Mahatma fasted until they ended, but twelve days after the end of his fast, he was suddenly and shockingly assassinated by a fanatic Hindu.

His death was regarded internationally as an enormous international tragedy. His contribution to history was monumental. His unique achievement of gaining independence for his country was hailed universally. The influence of this great soul continues to this day to inspire all those struggling for independence from tyranny. His example of how to lead a truly religious and spiritual life was a shining beacon of inspiration all over the world, and remains so until this day.

Alan Jacobs

Part One

Extracts from *Collected Works*

CHAPTER 1

Early Days And The
South African Struggle

LETTER TO FREDERICK LELY
London, December 1888

Dear Sir,

You will know me by looking at the note which, you said, when I had the opportunity of seeing you, you would preserve. At that time I had requested you to render to me some pecuniary aid as a means to enable me to proceed to England; but unfortunately you were in a hurry to leave; so I had not the sufficient time to say all that I had to say. I was at that time very impatient to proceed to England. So I left India on the 4th of September, 1888, with what little money I had at that time. What my father left for us three brothers was indeed very little. However, trusting that nearly £666, which was all my brother could with great difficulty spare for me, would be sufficient for my three years' stay in London, I left India for receiving legal education in England. I knew while in India that education and living in London were very expensive. But now from two months' experience in London, I find that they are more so than they appeared to be in India. In order to live here comfortably and to receive good education, I shall require an extra help of £400. I am a native of Porbandar and as such that is the only place I can look up to for such help.

During the late rule of H. H. the Rana Saheb, very little encouragement was given to education. But we can naturally expect that education must be encouraged under the English Administration. I am one who can take advantage of such encouragement. I hope, therefore, that you may please render me some pecuniary help and thereby confer great and much-needed obligation on me. I have asked my brother Laxmidas Gandhi to receive [it] and am sending him a note to see you in person if necessary.

Trusting you will be induced to grant my request.

With best respects,

I beg to remain, yours,

M. K. Gandhi

SPEECH TO THE BAND OF MERCY
Upper Norwood, London
Reported in *The Vegetarian*, 6 June 1891

By previous arrangement … Mrs. McDouall … was to deliver a lecture to a meeting of the members of the Band of Mercy, by the courtesy of Miss Seecombe, but she being ill, Mr. Gandhi (a Hindu from India) was requested and kindly consented to take the meeting. Mr. Gandhi spoke for about a quarter of an hour on vegetarianism from a humanitarian standpoint, and insisted that the members of the Band of Mercy, in order to be logical, ought to be vegetarian. He wound up with a quotation from Shakespeare.

LETTER TO THE PROTHONOTARY AND REGISTRAR OF THE HIGH COURT OF JUDICATURE

Bombay, 17 June 1897

Sir,

I am desirous of being admitted as an Advocate of the High Court. I was called to the Bar in England on the 10th June last. I have kept twelve terms in the Inner Temple and I intend to practise in the Bombay Presidency. I produce the certificate of my being called to the Bar. As to the certificate of my character and abilities, I have not been able to obtain any certificate from a judge in England, for I was not aware of the rules in force in the Bombay High Court. I, however, produce a certificate from Mr. W. D. Edwards, a practising Barrister in the Supreme Court of Judicature in England. He is the author of the *Compendium of the Law of Property in Land*, one of the books prescribed for the Bar Final Examination.

I beg to remain, Sir;

Your most obedient servant

M. K. Gandhi

FROM A LETTER FOLLOWING A
JOURNEY ON A SHIP FROM ENGLAND
TO BOMBAY (ON WHICH FOOD WAS
SERVED IN PLENTIFUL AMOUNTS)
30 November 1891

Your belly is your God, your stomach is your temple, your paunch is your altar, your cook is your priest … . It is in the cooking-pots that your love is inflamed, it is in the kitchen that your faith grows fervid, it is in the flesh-dishes that all hope lies hid … . Who is held in so much esteem with you as the frequent giver of dinners, as the sumptuous entertainer, as the practised toaster of health?

FROM A LETTER TO THE EDITOR OF
THE NATAL ADVERTISER (REGARDING
AN INCIDENT THAT WAS REPORTED
IN *THE NATAL MERCURY*)
Durban, 26 May 1893

Sir,

I was startled to read a paragraph in your today's issue referring to myself, under the heading, 'An Unwelcome Visitor'.

'An Indian entered the Court House yesterday afternoon and took a seat at the horseshoe. He was well-dressed and it was understood that he was an English barrister, on his way to Pretoria, where he is reported to be engaged in an Indian case. He entered the Court without removing his head-covering or salaaming, and the Magistrate looked at him with disapproval. The new arrival was courteously asked his business, and he replied that he was an English barrister. He did not attempt to present his credentials, and, on returning to the horseshoe was quietly told that the proper course for him to pursue, before taking up his position at the Bar, was to gain admission to the Supreme Court.'

PETITION TO NATAL
LEGISLATIVE ASSEMBLY
Durban, 28 June 1894

To the Honourable Speaker and Members of the Legislative Assembly of the colony of Natal

The petition of the Indians resident in the colony of Natal humbly sheweth that:

1 Your Petitioners are British subjects, who have come from India and settled in the Colony.

2 Your Petitioners are many of them registered as electors duly qualified to vote at the election of members to your Honourable Council and Assembly.

3 Your Petitioners have read with feelings of unfeigned regret and alarm the debate as reported in the newspapers on the second reading of the Franchise Law Amendment Bill.

4 Your Petitioners, with the greatest deference to your Honourable House, beg to dissent entirely from the views of the various speakers, and feel constrained to say that the real facts fail to support the reasons adduced in justification of the passing of the unfortunate measure.

5 The reasons, as reported in the newspapers, brought forward in support of the measure, your Petitioners understand, are: (a) that the Indians have never exercised the franchise in the land they come from; (b) that they are not fit for the exercise of the franchise.

6 Your Petitioners respectfully beg to press on the notice of the Honourable Members that all the facts and history point the other way.

7 The Indian nation has known, and has exercised, the power of election from times far prior to the time when the Anglo-Saxon races first became acquainted with the principles of representation.

DEPUTATION TO NATAL GOVERNOR
Durban, 3 July 1894

To his Excellency the Honourable Sir Walter Francis
Hely-Hutchinson, K.C.M.G., Governor and Commander-
in-Chief in and over the colony of Natal, Vice-Admiral of
the same, and Supreme Chief over the native population

May it please your Excellency,

At a meeting held on the 1st July, 1894, of leading Indians
in Durban, we were requested to await Your Excellency's
pleasure with regard to the Franchise Law Amendment Bill,
which was read a third time last evening in the Honourable
the Legislative Assembly of the Colony of Natal.

The Bill as it stands, disqualifies every Indian, whether
a British subject or not, not already on the Voters' List,
from becoming a voter. We venture to say that, without any
further qualification, the Bill is manifestly unjust, and would
work very harshly at any rate upon some Indians. Even in
England, any British subject having the proper qualifica-
tions is entitled to vote, irrespective of caste, colour, or creed.

We would not deal at length with the question here
lest we should trespass too much upon Your Excellency's
courtesy, but would beg leave to present Your Excellency
with a printed copy of the petition addressed to the
Honourable Assembly and request Your Excellency to
pursue it carefully. To us our cause seems to be so just that
it should not need any arguments to support it. We trust
that Your Excellency, representing Her Most Gracious
Majesty the Queen Empress, will not sanction a measure

that would seem to lay down that an Indian British subject of Her Majesty can never become fit to exercise the franchise.

BOOKS FOR SALE

Durban, before 26 November 1894

The following books by the late Mrs. Anna Kingsford and Mr. Edward Maitland are offered for sale at their published prices. They are introduced in South Africa for the first time:

The Perfect Way, 7/6
Clothed with the Sun, 7/6
The Story of the New Gospel of Interpretation, 2/6
The New Gospel of Interpretation, 1/-
The Bible's Own Account of Itself, 1/-

The following are some of the opinions concerning the books:
A fountain of light (*The Perfect Way*) interpretative and reconciliatory .... No student of divine things can dispense with it.

– *Light*, London

Unequalled as a means of grace amongst all the English books of the century.

– *Occult World*

Some pamphlets bearing on the subject can be had free of charge at my office.

M. K. Gandhi
Agent for the Esoteric Christian Union and the London Vegetarian Society

FROM *THE SONG CELESTIAL*
BY SIR EDWIN ARNOLD
[a poetic rendition of the Bhagavad Gita *that Mahatma Gandhi admired greatly and often quoted]*:

'What the wise choose the unwise people take;

What the best men do the multitude will follow.'

Another favourite was a quotation from a letter of the late Abbe Constant:

'Humanity has always and everywhere asked itself these three supreme questions: Whence come we? What are we? Whither go we?'

OPEN LETTER, DURBAN

before 19 December 1894

To the Hon. Members of the Hon. the Legislative Council and the Hon. the Legislative Assembly

Sirs,

Were it possible to write to you anonymously, nothing would have been more pleasing to me. But the statements I shall have to make in this letter will be so grave and important that it would be considered a sheer act of cowardice not to disclose my name. I beg, however, to assure you that I write not from selfish motives, nor yet from those of self-aggrandisement or of seeking notoriety. The one and only object is to serve India, which is by accident of birth called my native country, and to bring about better understanding between the European section of the community and the Indian in this Colony. The only way this can be done is to appeal to those who represent and, at the same time, mould public opinion.

Hence, if the Europeans and the Indians live in a perpetual state of quarrel, the blame would lie on your shoulders. If both can walk together and live together quietly and without friction, you will receive great benefit.

M. K. Gandhi

[The following passages were quoted by Gandhi in his *Franchise Petition*, 1894.]

PRACTICAL RELIGION IN INDIA

As to Indian philosophy and religion, the learned author of the book *The Indian Empire* thus sums it up this way. 'The Brahmin solutions to the problems of practical religion are self discipline, alms, sacrifice to and contemplation of the Deity. But, besides the practical questions of the spiritual life, religion has also intellectual problems, such as the compatibility of evil with the goodness of God, and the unequal distribution of happiness and misery in this life. Brahmin philosophy has exhausted the possible solutions of these difficulties, and of most of the other great problems which have since perplexed the Greek and Roman sage, mediaeval schoolman and modern men of science'.

The various hypotheses of creation, arrangement and development were each elaborated and the views of physiologists at the present day are a return with new lights to the evolution theory of Kapila. The works on religion published in the native language in India in 1877 numbered 1192, besides 56 on mental and moral philosophy. In 1882 the total had risen to 1545 on religion and 153 on mental and moral philosophy.

If I were asked under what sky the human mind has most fully developed some of its choicest gifts, has most deeply pondered on the greatest problems of life, and has found solutions of some of them which well deserve the attention even of those who have studied Plato and Kant – I should point to India; and if I were to ask myself from what literature we have here in Europe, we who have been nurtured almost exclusively on the thoughts of Greeks and Romans, and of one Semitic race, the Jews, may draw that corrective which is most wanted in order to make our inner life more perfect, more comprehensive, more universal, in fact, more truly human – a life not for this life only, but a transfigured and eternal life – again I should point to India. The German philosopher, Schopenhauer, thus adds his testimony to the grandeur of Indian philosophy as contained in the Upanishads:

'From every sentence deep, original and sublime thoughts arise, and the whole is pervaded by a high and holy and earnest spirit. Indian air surrounds us, and original thoughts of kindred spirits ... In the whole world there is no study, except that of the originals, so beneficial and so elevating as that of the Upanishads. It has been the solace of my life; it will be the solace of my Death.'

SCIENCE IN INDIA

Coming to science, Sir William Jones says 'The science of language, indeed, had been reduced in India to fundamental principles at a time when the grammarians of the West still treated it on the basis of accidental resemblances, and modern philosophy dates from the study of Sanskrit by European scholars ... The grammar of Panini stands supreme among the grammars of the world ... It arranges in logical harmony the whole phenomena which the Sanskrit language presents, and stands forth as one of the most splendid achievements of human invention and industry.'

Speaking on the same department of science, Sir H. S. Maine, in his Rede lecture, published in the latest edition of the *Village-Communities*, says: 'India has given to the world Comparative Philosophy and Comparative Mythology; it may yet give us a new science not less valuable than the sciences of language and of folklore. I hesitate to call it Comparative Jurisprudence because, if it ever exists, its area will be so much wider than the field of law. For India not only contains (or to speak more accurately, did contain) an Aryan language older than any other descendant of the common mother tongue, and a variety of names of natural objects less perfectly crystallized than elsewhere into fabulous personages, but it includes a whole world of Aryan institutions, Aryan customs, Aryan laws Aryan ideas, Aryan, beliefs, in a far earlier stage of growth and development than any which survive beyond its borders.'

Of Indian astronomy the same historian says: 'The astronomy of the Brahmins has formed alternately the subject of excessive admiration and of misplaced contempt ... In certain points the Brahmins advanced beyond Greek astronomy. Their fame spread throughout the West, and found entrance into the Chronicon Paschale. In the 8th and 9th centuries the Arabs became their disciples. I again quote Sir William: 'In algebra and arithmetic the Brahmins attained a high degree of proficiency independent of Western aid. To them we owe the invention of the numerical symbols on the decimal system ... The Arabs borrowed these figures from the Hindus, and transmitted them to Europe ... The works on mathematics and mechanical science, published in the native languages in India in 1867, numbered 89, and in 1882, 166.'

'The medical science of the Brahmins', continues the eminent historian, 'was also an independent development ... . The specific diseases whose names occur in Panini's grammar indicate that medical studies had made progress before his time (350 BC) ... . Arabic medicine was founded on the translations from the Sanskrit treatises ... . European medicine down to the 17th century was based upon the Arabic ... . The number of medical works published in the native languages of India in 1877 amounted to 130, and in 1882 to 212, besides 87 on natural science.'

Writing of the art of war, the writer proceeds: 'The Brahmins regarded not only medicine but also the arts of war, music, and architecture as supplementary parts of their divinely inspired knowledge ... . The Sanskrit epics prove that strategy had attained to the position of a recognized science before the birth of Christ, and the later Agni Purana devotes long sections to its systematic treatment.'

THE ARTS IN INDIA

The Indian art of music was destined to exercise a wider influence ... . This notation passed from the Brahmins through the Persians to Arabia, and was thence introduced into European music by Guido Arezzo at the beginning of the 11th century. On architecture the Sir William says: 'The Buddhists were the great stone-builders of India. Their monasteries and shrines exhibit the history of the art during twenty-two centuries, from the earliest cave structures of the rock temples to the latest Jain erections dazzling in stucco, over-crowded with ornament. It seems not improbable that the churches of Europe owe their steeples to the Buddhist topes ... . Hindu art has left memorials which extort the admiration and astonishment of our age.

The Hindu palace architecture of Gwalior, the Indian Mahommedan mosques, the mausoleums of Agra and Delhi, with several of the older Hindu temples of Southern India, stand unrivalled for grace of outline and elaborate wealth of ornament.

English decorative art in our day has borrowed largely from Indian forms and patterns ... . Indian art works, when faithful to native designs, still obtain the highest honours at the international exhibitions of Europe.'

Here is what Andrew Carnegie in his *Round the World* says about the Taj of Agra:

'There are some subjects too sacred for analysis, or even for words. And I now know that there is a human structure so exquisitely fine or unearthly, as to lift it into this holy domain ... . The Taj is built of a light creamy marble, so that it does not chill one as pure cold white marble does. It is warm and sympathetic as a woman ... . One great critic has freely called the Taj a feminine structure. There is nothing masculine about it, says he; its charms are all feminine. This creamy marble is inlaid with fine black marble lines, the entire Koran, in Arabic letters, it is said, being thus interwoven … Till the day I die, amid mountain streams or moonlight strolls in the forest, wherever and whenever the moon comes, when all that is most sacred, most elevated and most pure recur to shed their radiance upon the tranquil mind, there will be found among my treasures the memory of that lovely charm—the Taj.'

Nor has India been without its laws, codified or otherwise. The Institutes of Manu have always been noted for their justice and precision. So much does Sir H. S. Maine seem to have been struck with their equity that he calls them 'an ideal picture of that which, in the view of the Brahmins, ought to be the law'. Mr. Pincott, writing in 1891 in *The National Review*, alludes to them as 'the philosophical laws of Manu'.

THE DRAMATIC ARTS IN INDIA

Nor have the Indians been deficient in the dramatic art. Goethe thus speaks of *Shakuntala*, the most famous Indian drama:

> 'Wouldst thou the young year's blossoms, and the
>   fruits of its decline,
> And all by which the soul is charmed, enraptured,
>   feasted, fed.
> Wouldst thou the earth, and heaven itself in one
>   sole name combine?
> I name thee, O Shakuntala! and all at once is said.'

INDIAN SOCIAL LIFE

Coming to the Indian character and social life, the evidence is voluminous. I can only give meagre extracts. I take the following again from Hunter's *Indian Empire*: The Greek ambassador (Megasthenes) observed with admiration the absence of slavery in India, and the chastity of the women and the courage of the men. In valour they excelled all other Asiatics; they required no locks to their doors; above all, no Indian was ever known to tell a lie. Sober and industrious, good farmers and skilful artisans, they scarcely ever had recourse to a lawsuit, and lived peaceably under their native chiefs. The kingly government is portrayed almost as described in Manu, with its hereditary castes of councillors and soldiers ... The village system is well described, each little rural unit *seeming to the Greek an independent republic.*

THE PEOPLE OF INDIA

Bishop Heber says of the people of India: 'So far as their natural character is concerned, I have been led to form on the whole a very favourable opinion. They are men of high and gallant courage, courteous, intelligent, and most eager after knowledge and improvement ... They are sober, industrious, dutiful to their parents, and affectionate to their children; of tempers almost uniformly gentle and patient, and more easily affected by kindness and attention to their wants and feelings than almost any men whom I have met with.'

Sir Thomas Munro, sometime Governor of Madras, says:

'I do not exactly know what is meant by civilizing the people of India. In the theory and practice of good government they may be deficient, but if a good system of agriculture, if unrivalled manufacturers, if a capacity to produce what convenience and luxury demand, if the establishment of schools for reading and writing, if the general practice of kindness and hospitality, and, above all, if a scrupulous respect and delicacy towards the female sex, are amongst the points that denote a civilized people, then the Hindus are not inferior in civilization to the people of Europe.'

THE CHARACTER OF THE INDIANS

They are long-suffering and patient, hardy and enduring, frugal and industrious, law-abiding and peace-seeking … The educated and higher mercantile classes are honest and truthful, and loyal and trustful towards the British Government, in the most absolute sense that I can use, and you understand the words. Moral truthfulness is as marked a characteristic of the Settia (upper) class of Bombay as of the Teutonic race itself. The people of India, in short, are in no intrinsic sense our inferiors, while in things measured by some of the false standards – false to our-selves – we pretend to believe in, they are our superiors.

Sri C. Trevelyan remarks that: 'They have very considerable administrative qualities, great patience, industry, and great acuteness and intelligence.'

Of the family relations, thus speaks Sir W. W. Hunter:

'There is simply no comparison between Englishmen and Hindus with respect to the place occupied by family interests and family affections in their minds. The love of parents for children and of children for parents has scarcely any counterpart in England. Parental and filial affection among our Eastern fellow-citizens occupies the place which is taken in this country by the passion between the sexes.'

And Mr. Pincott thinks that: 'In all social matters the English are far more fitted to sit at the feet of Hindus and learn as disciples than to attempt to become masters.'

Says M. Louis Jacolliot: 'Soil of ancient India, cradle of humanity, hail! Hail, venerable and efficient nurse, whom centuries of brutal invasions have not yet buried under the dust of oblivion. Hail, fatherland of faith, of love, of poetry, and of science! May we hail a revival of thy past in our Western future!'

Says Victor Hugo: 'These nations have made Europe, France and Germany. Germany is for the Occident that which India is for the Orient.

Add to this the facts that India has produced a Buddha, whose life some consider the best and the holiest lived by a mortal, and some to be second only to that lived by Jesus.'

THE SITUATION OF INDIANS IN NATAL

They come to Natal on starvation wages (I mean here the indentured Indians). They find themselves placed in a strange position and amid uncongenial surroundings. The moment they leave India they remain throughout life, if they settle in the Colony, without any moral education. Whether they are Hindus or Mahommedans, they are absolutely without any moral or religious instruction worthy of the name. They have not learned enough to educate themselves without any outside help. Placed thus, they are apt to yield to the slightest temptation to tell a lie. After some time, lying with them becomes a habit and a disease. They would lie without any reason, without any prospect of bettering themselves materially, indeed, without knowing what they are doing. They reach a stage in life when their moral faculties have completely collapsed owing to neglect. There is also a very sad form of lying. They cannot dare tell the truth, even for their wantonly ill-treated brother, for fear of receiving ill-treatment from their master. They are not philosophic enough to look with equanimity on the threatened reduction in their miserable rations and serve corporal punishment, did they dare to give evidence against their master. Are these men, then, more to be despised than pitied? Are they to be treated as scoundrels, deserving no mercy, or are they to be treated as helpless creatures, badly in need of sympathy? Is there any class of people who would not do as they are doing under similar circumstances?

AN OPEN LETTER TO EUROPEANS
Beach Grove, Durban, 19 December 1894

Sir

I venture to send you the enclosed for perusal, and solicit your opinion on the subject matter of the Open Letter. Whether you be a clergyman, editor, public man, merchant or lawyer, the subject cannot but demand your attention. If you are a clergyman, inasmuch as you represent the teaching of Jesus, it must be your duty to see that you are in no way, directly or indirectly, countenancing a treatment of your fellow-beings that would not be pleasing to Jesus. If you are an editor of a news-paper, the responsibility is equally great. Whether you are using your influence as a journalist to the evolution or degradation of humanity will depend upon whether you are encouraging division among class and class or striving after union. The same remarks will apply to you as a public man. If you are a merchant or lawyer, you have then too, a duty to discharge towards your customers and clients from whom you derive a considerable pecuniary advantage. It is for you to treat them as dogs or fellow-beings demanding your sympathy in the cruel persecution that they are put to owing to the prevalent ignorance about the Indians in the Colony. Coming as you do in comparatively close contact with them, you have, no doubt, the opportunity and incentive to study them. Looked at from a sympathetic standpoint, they would perhaps show themselves to you as they have been seen by scores and hundreds of Europeans who had the opportunity to study them, and who used it alright. Your opinion is solicited with a view to ascertaining if there are many Europeans in the Colony who would actively sympathize with and feel for the Indians in the Colony, assuming that their treatment is not all that could be desired.

I am, Sir,

Your faithful servant,

M. K. Gandhi

LETTER TO HIS HONOUR THE STATE PRESIDENT OF THE SOUTH AFRICAN REPUBLIC, PRETORIA

May it please your Honour:

In view of the gross misrepresentation by certain interested Europeans residing in the Republic, to the effect that the burghers of this State are opposed to the Indians residing or trading in the State, and their agitation against these people, we, the undersigned burghers, beg respectfully to state that so far from the burghers being opposed to these people fully stopping and trading in the State, they recognize in them a peaceful and law-abiding, and therefore desirable, class of people. To the poor they are a veritable blessing inasmuch as by their keen competition they keep down the prices of necessaries of life which they can do owing to their thrifty and temperate habits.

We venture to submit that their withdrawal from the State will be a dire calamity to us, especially those of us who, living far away from centres of business, depend upon the Indians for the supply of our daily wants, and that therefore any measures restrictive of their freedom, and having for their object their ultimate removal, and especially that of those Indians who are traders and hawkers, will necessarily interfere with our enjoyment and comforts. We, therefore, humbly pray that the Government will not take any steps that may scare away the Indians from the Transvaal.

[Signed by a number of Burghers]

PETITION[1] TO LORD ELGIN
before 5 May 1895

To His Excellency the Right Honourable the Earl of Elgin, P.C., G.M.S.I., G.M.I.E., etc., etc.
Viceroy and Governor-General of India
Calcutta

The petition of the undersigned Indians residing in the South African Republic humbly sheweth that:

Your Petitioners representing the Indian community in the South African Republic venture hereby to approach Your Excellency with regard to Her Majesty's Indian British subjects in the South African Republic.

Your Petitioners instead of reiterating the facts and

arguments embodied in a similar petition[2], signed by over 10,000 British Indians, and sent to the Right Honourable the Secretary of State for the Colonies, beg to append hereto a copy of the petition with its annexures, and commend it to Your Excellency's perusal. Your Petitioners after mature deliberation have come to the conclusion that unless they sought the direct protection of Your Excellency as Her Majesty's representative and virtual Ruler of all India, and unless that protection was graciously accorded, the position of the Indians in the South African Republic, and indeed throughout the whole of South Africa, would be utterly helpless and the enterprising Indians in South Africa would be forcibly degraded to the position of the Natives of South Africa, and this through no fault of their own. If an intelligent stranger were to visit the South African Republic, and were told that there was a class of people in South Africa who could not hold fixed property, who could not move about the State without passes, who alone had to pay a special registration

---

[1] This petition, along with the preceding item, was forwarded by Sir Jacobus de Wet on May 30, 1895, to the High Commissioner, Cape Town.

[2] May 1895 petition to Lord Rippon

A BAND OF VEGETARIAN MISSIONARIES

It was in England that I read in Mrs. Anna Kingsford's *Perfect Way in Diet* that there was a colony of Trappists in South Africa who were vegetarians. Ever since that I had wished to see these vegetarians. The wish has at last been realized. At the outset, I may remark that South Africa, and particularly Natal, is especially adapted for vegetarians. The Indians have made Natal the Garden Colony of South Africa. One can grow almost anything on the South African soil, and that in abundance. The supply of bananas, pineapples and oranges is almost inexhaustible, and far greater than the demand. There is no wonder that the vegetarians can thrive very well in Natal.

REPORT OF THE NATAL INDIAN CONGRESS
August 1895

ITS FOUNDATION

During the month of June in the year 1894 the Natal Government introduced a Bill called the Franchise Law Amendment Bill in the Legislative Assembly. It was recognized that it threatened the very existence of the Indians in the Colony. Meetings were held on the premises of Messrs Dada Abdulla & Co. to consider what steps should be taken to prevent the Bill from passing. Petitions were sent to both the Houses, Members of which were interviewed by a representative who went from Durban to P.M. Burg. The Bill, however, passed both the Houses. The effect of the agitation was that all the Indians recognized the absolute necessity of establishing a permanent institution that would cope with the legislative activity, of a retrograde character, of the first Responsible Government of the Colony with regard to the Indians, and protect Indian interests.

After a few preliminary meetings had been held on Messrs Dada Abdulla's premises, the Natal Indian Congress was formally established on the 22nd August amidst great enthusiasm. All the leading members of the Indian community joined the Congress. Seventy-six members subscribed on the first evening.

VEGETARIANISM IN NATAL
(a speech at a public meeting in Bombay)

It is an uphill battle to fight in Natal, and, indeed, in South Africa. Yet there are few places where vegetarianism would be more conducive to health, or more economical or practicable. Of course, at present, it is hardly economical and it certainly requires a great deal of self-denial to remain a vegetarian. To become one seems almost an impossibility. 'It is all very well in London, where there are scores of vegetarian restaurants, but how can you become or remain a vegetarian in South Africa, where you find very little nourishing vegetarian food?' has been the invariable reply to my enquiries, in the course of conversation on the matter with scores of men. One would have thought such a reply would be impossible in South Africa, seeing that it enjoys a semi-tropical climate, and its vegetable resources are inexhaustible. Nevertheless, the reply is entirely justifiable. In the best of hotels you find, as a rule, potatoes the only vegetable at lunch-time, and that badly cooked. At dinner-time you find, perhaps, two vegetables, and the vegetable menu is hardly ever changed. It is little short of a scandal that in this Garden Colony of South Africa, where, at the proper time, you can get fruit for a song, that such a situation exists.

26 SEPTEMBER 1896

I stand before you, today, as representing the signatories to this document, who pose as representative of the 100,000 British Indians at present residing in South Africa – a country which has sprung into sudden prominence owing to the vast gold fields of Johannesburg and the late Jameson Raid. This is my sole qualification. I am a person of few words. The cause, however, for which I am to plead before you this evening is so great that I venture to think that you will overlook the faults of the speaker or, rather, the reader of this paper. The interests of 100,000 Indians are closely bound up with the interests of the 300 millions of India. The question of the grievances of the Indians in South Africa affects the future well-being and the future immigration of Indians of India. I, therefore, humbly venture to think that this question should be, if it is not already, one of the questions of the day in India.

LETTER OF 13 OCTOBER 1896

I leave for Madras tomorrow. I expect to stay there not more than a fortnight. If I am successful there I would thence proceed to Calcutta and return to Bombay within a month from today. I would then take the first boat to Natal. The latest papers received from Natal show that there is still much fight ahead. I am sure it is a cause worth fighting for.

SPEECH AT FAREWELL MEETING IN DURBAN, 15 OCTOBER 1901
(reported in *The Natal Advertiser*, 16 October 1901)

[On the eve of his departure for India, Gandhiji was presented with addresses; on behalf of the Natal Indian Congress and other Indian organizations. The large gathering in the Congress Hall, Durban, included several

leading European citizens. The following is a brief report
of the speech Gandhiji made on the occasion:]

Mr. Gandhi returned thanks from the bottom of his heart
for the splendid and costly address. He thanked the donors
of the many presents; and also those who had spoken so
flatteringly of him. He had not been able to find a satisfac-
tory answer to the question of how he came to deserve all
this. Seven or eight years ago, they embarked on a certain
principle, and he accepted the gifts as an earnest [indication]
that they would continue on the lines on which they then
embarked. The Natal Indian Congress had worked to bring
about a better understanding between European and Indian
Colonists. They had progressed in that, if only a little way.
During the recent election speeches they heard much
against the Indians. What was wanted in South Africa was
not a white man's country; not a white brotherhood, but
an Imperial brotherhood. Everyone who was the friend of
the Empire should aim at that. England would never part
with her possession in the East, and, as Lord Curzon had
said, India was the brightest jewel in the British Empire.
They wished to show that they were an acceptable section of
the community, and, if they continued as they started, they
'would know each other better when the mists have rolled
away. Mr. Gandhi then addressed the Indians in their native
language, and the meeting terminated with cheers for their
distinguished countryman.

ADDRESS SENT TO GANDHI
15 October 1901

To Mohandas Karamchand Gandhi, Esq., Barrister-at-Law, Honorary Secretary, Natal Indian Congress, &c., &c.

Sir,

We, the undersigned, representing all classes of Indians living in Natal, beg leave to present this Address to you on the eve of your departure for India, to very briefly express, howsoever poorly, the deep sense of gratitude we entertain towards you for the valuable services you have so untiringly and cheerfully rendered, and the exemplary self-sacrifice you have ever-willingly undergone to watch and further the interests of your fellow-countrymen since your arrival in the Colony over eight years ago.

Your unique career teaches many a luminous lesson, and we hope to model our actions by the noble example set by you. In all you did you were guided by high ideals, and your unflinching devotion to duty made your methods and work most efficient. We feel that in honouring you we honour ourselves. We sincerely hope that after discharging the domestic duties that necessitate your going to India, you will decide to cast your lot with us again, and continue the work you have been so admirably doing.

In conclusion, we wish you *bon voyage*, and pray to the Almighty to confer His choicest blessings on you and yours.

We beg to remain, Sir, Ever yours gratefully,

Abdul Cadir [and others]

CHAPTER 2

The Indian Struggle

REPORT IN *MADRAS TIMES*
15 April 1915

Mr. Gandhi did return to South Africa again to continue his struggle there, but in 1915, on his last return to India from South Africa, he began his preparation for his campaign to eventually free India from British Rule.

Questioned as to his future work in India, Mr. Gandhi said he had been touring round the country as was advised for study, preliminary to forming a definite plan of work in the service of the country.

ADVICE TO ASPIRANTS
(in a fragment of a letter to Mathuradas Trikumj)
7 February 1915

Truthfulness, *brahmacharya*, non-violence, non-stealing and non-hoarding, these five rules of life are obligatory on all aspirants. Everyone should be an aspirant. A man's character, therefore, is to be built on the foundation of these disciplines. Beyond doubt, they are to be observed by everyone in the world. Though a business man, one must never utter or practise untruth; though married, one must remain celibate; though keeping oneself alive, one can practise non-violence. It is difficult to be of the world and yet not to steal (to observe the rule of non-stealing) and not to hoard wealth or any other thing. One must, nevertheless, keep that as an ideal to be attained and have some limit in these respects; when the mind has begun to turn away from these things, one may even embrace the supreme renunciation. Everyone who observes these vows will be able to find a way out of all perplexities.

LETTER TO MAGANLAL GANDHI
after 14 March 1915

You are right in what you think about non-violence. Its essentials are *daya* [compassion], *akrodha* [freedom from anger], *aman* [freedom from the desire to be respected] etc. Satyagraha [the political struggle] is based on non-violence. We saw this clearly in Calcutta and came to the conclusion that we should include it among our vows. The thought led to the further conclusion that we must observe all the *yamas*[1] and that, if we do so by way of vows, we perceive the inner significance of non-violence. In my talks with hundreds of men here I place the various *yamas* above everything else.

I remembered a verse in Calcutta on this occasion and pondered deeply over it. I am absolutely clear in my mind that India's deliverance and ours will be achieved through the observance of these vows. In observing the vow of non-hoarding, the main thing to be borne in mind is not to store up anything which we do not require.

Any great moral or religious duty or observance. The *yamas* are usually said to be ten, but their names are given differently by different writers. Generally they include truth-fulness, non-violence, compassion, celibacy, etc.

FROM A SPEECH AT THE YMCA, MADRAS
(referring to Bankim Chandra Chatterji,the author of the
words of the hymn *The Vande Mataram*) April 1915

He describes Mother India as sweet-smelling, sweet-speak-ing, fragrant, all-powerful, all-good, truthful, a land flowing with milk and honey, and having ripe fields, fruits and grains, and inhabited by a race of men of whom we have only a picture in the great Golden Age. He pictures to us a land which shall embrace in its possession the whole of the world, the whole of humanity by the might or right not of physical power but of soul-power. Can we sing that hymn? I ask myself, 'Can I, by any right, spring to my feet when I listen to that song?' The poet no doubt gave us a picture for our realisation the words of which simply remain prophetic, and it is for you, the hope of India, to realise every word that the poet has said in describing this Motherland of ours…. It is for you and for me to make good the claim that the poet has advanced on behalf of our Motherland.

SPEECH AT A RECEPTION AT
TRANQUEBAR, 30 APRIL 1915
The Hindu, 1 May 1915

Yesterday the public of Tranquebar and suburbs accorded a grand and enthusiastic reception to Mr. and Mrs. Gandhi. Over 2,000 people representing numerous classes, particularly passive resisters, had assembled … .Mr. K. C. Subramaniam, Barrister, read the welcome address … .

The distinguished guest replied in appropriate terms exhorting his fellow-workers to take to passive resistance whenever and wherever needed for adopting constitutional agitation [*sic*]. His speech was heard with rapt attention and it was translated on the spot. The Hon'ble Mr. V. S. Srinivasa Sastri was next called upon to speak. He exhorted the audience to work for their country's cause.

SPEECH ON 'UNTOUCHABLES'
AT MAYAVARAM
1 May 1915

I have now to learn what Hinduism really is. In so far as I have been able to study Hinduism outside India, I have felt that it is no part of real Hinduism to have in its hold a mass of people whom I would call 'untouchables'. If it was proved to me that this is an essential part of Hinduism, I for one would declare myself an open rebel against Hinduism itself.

('Hear, hear.') But I am still not convinced and I hope that up to the end of my life, I shall remain unconvinced that it is an essential part of Hinduism. But who is responsible for this class of untouchables? I have been told that wherever there are Brahmins, it is they who are enjoying supremacy as a matter of right, but today are they enjoying that supremacy? If they are, then the sin will fall upon their shoulders and that is the return I am here to declare and that is the return I shall have to make for the kindness you are showing to me; often my love to my friends, relations and even to my dear wife takes devious ways. So my return here for your kindness is to suggest a few words which you were probably not prepared to listen to and it does seem to me that it is high time for Brahmins to regain their natural prerogative. I recall to my mind the beautiful verse in the *Bhagavad Gita*. I shall not excite the audience by reciting the verse, but give you simply a paraphrase. 'The true Brahmin is he who is equi-minded towards a Pundit and a Pariah.' Are the Brahmins in Mayavaram equi-minded?

SPEECH AT BANGALORE
1 May 1915

Modern civilization a curse

Modern civilization is a curse in Europe as also in India. War is the direct result of modern civilization. Every one of the powers was making preparations for war.

Great moral force

Passive resistance is a great moral force meant for the weak, also for the strong. Soul-force depends on itself. Ideals must work in practice, otherwise they are not potential. Modern civilization is brute force.

It is one thing to know the ideal and another thing to practise it. That will ensure greater discipline, which means greater service and greater service means greater gain to Government. Passive resistance is a high aggressive thing. The attribute of soul is restlessness; there is room for every phase of thought.

Three evils

Money, land and woman are the sources of evil and evil has to be counteracted. I need not possess land, nor a woman, nor money, to satisfy my luxuries. I do not want to be unhinged because others are unhinged. If ideals are practised, there will be less room for mischievous activities. Public life has to be moulded.

DRAFT CONSTITUTION
FOR THE ASHRAM
before 20 May 1915

Object

The object of the Ashram is to learn how to serve the motherland one's whole life and how to serve the Ashram.

Classes

The Ashram consists of three classes: Controllers, Novitiates and Students.

(1) Controllers

The Controllers believe that, in order to learn how to serve the country, the following observance should be enforced in their own lives and they have been trying to do so for some time.

1. *Vow of truth*

   It is not enough for a person under this vow that he does not ordinarily resort to untruth; such a person ought to know that no deception may be practised even for the good of the country. One should consider the example of Prahlad in order to understand how one should behave towards elders such as parents in the interests of all.

2. *Vow of non-violence*

It is not enough to refrain from taking the life of any living being. He who has pledged himself to this vow may not kill even those whom he believes to be unjust; he may not be angry with them, he must love them; thus, he would oppose the tyranny whether of parents, governments or others, but will never kill or hurt the tyrant. The follower of truth and non-violence will offer satyagraha against tyranny and win over the tyrant by love; he will not carry out the tyrant's will but he will suffer punishment even unto death for disobeying his will until the tyrant himself is won over.

3. *Vow of celibacy*

It is well-nigh impossible to observe these two vows unless celibacy too is observed; and for this vow it is not enough that one does not look upon another woman with a lustful eye, one has so to control the animal passions that they will not be moved even in thought; if one is married, one will not have sexual intercourse even with one's wife, but, regarding her as a friend, will establish with her a relationship of perfect purity.

4. *Control of the palate*

Until one has overcome the palate, it is difficult to observe the foregoing vows, more especially that of celibacy. Control of the palate should therefore be treated as a separate observance by one desirous of serving the country and, believing that eating is only for sustaining the body, one should regulate and purify one's diet day by day. Such a person will immediately, or gradually, as he can, leave off such articles of food as may tend to stimulate animal passions.

5. Vow of non-stealing

It is not enough not to steal what is commonly considered as other men's property. One who has pledged himself to this vow should realize that Nature provides from day to day just enough and no more for one's daily needs by way of food and so hold it theft to use articles of food, dress etc., which one does not really need and live accordingly.

6. Vow of non-possession

It is not enough not to possess and keep much, but it is necessary not to keep anything which may not be absolutely necessary for the nourishment and protection of our body: thus, if one can do without chairs, one should do so. He who has taken this vow will always bear this in mind and endeavour to simplify his life more and more.

Subsidiary observances

Three other vows follow from the foregoing.

1. *Vow of Swadeshi*

The person who has taken the vow of swadeshi will never use articles which conceivably involve violation of truth in their manufacture or on the part of their manufacturers. It follows, for instance, that a votary of truth will not use articles manufactured in the mills of Manchester, Germany or India, for he cannot be sure that they involve no such violation of truth. Moreover, labourers suffer much in the mills. The generation of tremendous heat causes enormous destruction of life. Besides, the loss of workers' lives in the manufacture of machines and of other creatures through excessive heat is something impossible to describe. Foreign cloth and cloth made by means of machinery are, therefore, tabooed to a votary of non-violence as they involve triple violence. Further reflection will show that the use of foreign cloth can be held to involve a breach of the vows of non-stealing and non-possession. We follow custom and, for better appearance, wear foreign cloth in preference to the cloth made on our own handlooms with so little effort. Artificial beautifying of the body is a hindrance to a *brahmachari* and so, even from the point of view of that vow, machine-made cloth is taboo. Therefore, the vow of Swadeshi requires the use of simple clothing made on simple handlooms and stitched in simple style, foreign buttons, cuts, etc., being avoided. The same line of reasoning may be applied to all other articles.

2. Vow of fearlessness

He who is acted upon by fear can hardly observe the vows of truth, etc. The Controllers will, therefore, constantly endeavour to be free from the fear of kings or society, one's caste or family, thieves, robbers, ferocious animals such as tigers, and even of death. One who observes the vow of fearlessness will defend himself or others by truth-force or soul-force.

3. Vow against untouchability

According to Hindu religion as traditionally practised, communities such as Dhed, Bhangi, etc., known by the names of Antyaj, Pancham, Achhut and so on, are looked upon as untouchable. Hindus belonging to other communities believe that they will be defiled it they touch a member of any of the said communities and, if anyone does so accidentally, he thinks that he has committed a sin.

The founders of the Ashram believe that this practice is a blot on Hindu religion. Themselves staunch Hindus, they believe that the Hindu race will continue to add to its load of sin so long as it regards a single community as untouchable. Some of the consequences of this practice have been terrible. In order to be free from this sin, the Ashram inmates are under a vow to regard the untouchable communities as touchable;

actually one Dhed family was staying in the Ashram, and it is still there, when the third edition of these rules was being drawn up. It lives exactly in the same condition as others in the Ashram do. This vow does not extend to association for purpose of eating. All that is desired is the eradication of the evil of untouchability.

Varnashram

The Ashram does not follow the *varnashram* dharma. Where those in control of the Ashram will take the place of the pupils' parents and where life-long vows of celibacy, non-hoarding, etc., are to be observed, *varnashram* dharma has no scope. The Ashram inmates will be in the stage of *sanyasis* and so it is not necessary for them to follow the rules of this dharma. Apart from this, the Ashram has a firm belief in the *varnashram* dharma. The discipline of caste seems to have done no harm to the country; on the contrary, rather. There is no reason to believe that eating in company promotes brotherhood ever so slightly. In order that the *varnashram* dharma and caste discipline might in no way be undermined, the Ashram inmates are under obligation, whenever they stir out, to subsist on fruits if they cannot cook their own food. The organisation of society into four castes, each with a distinctive function, and the division of life into four stages.

Mother tongue

It is the belief of the Controllers that no nation or any group thereof can make real progress by abandoning its own language, they will, therefore, use their own language. As they desire to be on terms of intimacy with their brethren from all parts of India, they will also learn the chief Indian languages; as Sanskrit is a key to Indian languages, they will learn that too.

Manual work

The Controllers believe that body labour is a duty imposed by nature upon mankind. Such labour is the only means by which man may sustain himself; his mental and spiritual powers should be used for the common good only. As the vast majority in the world live on agriculture, the Controllers will always devote some part of their time to working on the land; when that is not possible, they will perform some other bodily labour.

Weaving

The Controllers believe that one of the chief causes of poverty in the land is the virtual disappearance of spinning-wheels and handlooms. They will, therefore, make every effort to revive this industry by themselves weaving cloth on handlooms.

Politics

Politics, economic progress etc., are not unconnected matters; knowing that they are all rooted in religion, the Controllers will make an effort to learn and teach politics, economics, social reform, etc., in a religious spirit and work in these fields with all the zeal that they can command.

(2) Novitiates

Those who are desirous of following the foregoing programme but are not able immediately to take the necessary vows may be admitted as Novitiates. It is obligatory upon them to conform to all the observances which are followed by Controllers the while that they are in the Ashram. They will acquire the status of Controllers when they are able to take the necessary vows for life.

(3) Students

1 Any children, whether boys or girls, from four years and upwards may be admitted with the consent of their parents.

2 Parents will have to surrender all control over their children.

3 Children will not be permitted to visit their parents for any reason until the whole course of study is finished.

4 Students will be taught to observe all the vows intended for the Controllers.

5 They will receive instruction in religion, agriculture, handloomweaving and letters.

6 Instruction in letters will be through the students' own languages and will include History, Geography, Arithmetic, Algebra, Geometry, Economics, etc., the learning of Sanskrit, Hindi and at least one Dravidian language being obligatory.

7 English will be taught as a second language.

8 Urdu, Bengali Tamil, Telugu, Devnagari and Gujarati scripts will be taught to all.

9 The Controllers believe that the whole course will be completed in ten years. Upon reaching the age of majority, students will be given the option of taking the vows or retiring from the Ashram. This will make it possible for those to whom the programme has not commended itself to leave the Ashram.

10 They will exercise this option at an age when they will require no assistance from their parents or guardians.

11 Every endeavour will be made from the very beginning to see that, when they leave, they will be strong enough to have no fear what they would do for their maintenance.

12 Grown-up persons also may be admitted as students.

13 As a rule, everyone will wear the simplest and a uniform style of dress.

14 Food will be simple. Chillies will be excluded altogether and generally no condiments will be used excepting salt, pepper and turmeric. Milk, ghee and other milk products being a hindrance to a celibate life and milk being often a cause of tuberculosis and having the same stimulating qualities as meat, they will be most sparingly used, if at all. Meals will be served thrice a day and will include dried and fresh fruits in liberal quantities. All inmates of the Ashram will be taught the general principles of hygiene.

15 No holidays will be observed in this Ashram but, for one and a half days every week, the ordinary routine will be altered and everyone will have some time to attend to his private work.

16 During three months in the year, those whose health permits it will be taken on a tour, on foot for the most part, of India.

17 Nothing will be charged either from Students or Novitiates towards their monthly expenditure, but parents or the members themselves will be expected to contribute whatever they can towards the expenses of the Ashram.

Miscellaneous

Administration of the Ashram will rest with a body of Controllers. The Chief Controller will have the right to decide whom to admit and to which category. The expenses of the Ashram are being met from moneys already received by the Chief Controller or to be received from friends who may have some faith in the Ashram. The Ashram is accommodated in two houses on the banks of the Sabarmati, Ahmedabad, on the road to Sarakhej across the Ellis Bridge. It is expected that in a few months, about 250 acres of land will be acquired in the vicinity of Ahmedabad and the Ashram located thereon.

A request

Visitors are requested to observe all the Ashram rules during their stay there. Every endeavour will be made to make them comfortable; but the management will be thankful to them if they bring with them their bedding and utensils for meals, as the Ashram rules permit the stocking of only a minimum of articles. Those parents who intend sending their children to the Ashram are advised to pay a visit to the Ashram. No boy or girl will be admitted before he or she has been duly tested.

Daily routine

(1) An effort is being made to see that everyone in the Ashram gets up at 4 o'clock. The first bell rings at 4.
(2) It is obligatory on all, except those who are ill, to get up at 4.30. Everyone finishes bathing by 5.
(3) 5 to 5.30: Prayers and readings from holy books.
(4) 5.30 to 7: Breakfast of fruits, such as bananas.
(5) 7 to 8.30: Manual work. This includes drawing water, grinding, sweeping, weaving cooking etc.
(6) 8.30 to 10: School work.
(7) 10 to 12: Meal and cleaning of utensils. The meal consists of dal, rice, vegetables and rotlis for five days. On two days, there are rotlis and fruits.
(8) 12 to 3: School work.
(9) 3 to 5: Work, as in the morning.
(10) 5 to 6: Meal and cleaning of utensils. The meal mostly follows the same pattern as in the morning.
(11) 6.30 to 7: Prayers, as in the morning.
(12) 7 to 9: Study, receiving visitors etc.
Before nine, all children go to bed. At ten the lights are put out.

For school work, the subjects of study at present are Sanskrit, Gujarati, Tamil, Hindi and Arithmetic. Study of History and Geography is included in that of languages.

No paid teachers or servants are employed in the Ashram. In all, the Ashram has at present 35 inmates. Four of them live with their families. There are five teachers to look after teaching. Permanent members of the Ashram include two from North India, nine from Madras Presidency and the rest are from Gujarat and Kathiawar.

RAMA AND RAVANA

Rama the soul and Ravana for the non-soul. The immense physical might of Ravana is as nothing compared to the soul-force of Rama. Ravana's ten heads are as straw to Rama. Rama is a yogi, he has conquered self and pride. He is 'placid equally in affluence and adversity', he has 'neither attachment, nor greed nor the intoxication of status'. This represents the ultimate in satyagraha. The banner of saytagraha can again fly in the Indian sky and it is our duty to raise it. If we take recourse to satyagraha, we can conquer our conquerors the English, make them bow before our tremendous soul-force, and the issue will be of benefit to the whole world. It is certain that India cannot rival Britain or Europe in force of arms. The British worship the war-god and they can all of them become, as they are becoming, bearers of arms. The hundreds of millions in India can never carry arms. They have made the religion of non-violence their own. It is impossible to fail.

LETTER TO VICEROY ON THE
PEACE CONFERENCE HELD AT
THE CLOSE OF WORLD WAR I
Delhi, 29 April 1918

Sir,

As you are aware, after careful consideration, I felt constrained to convey to Your Excellency that I could not attend the Conference for reasons stated in my letter of the 26th instant. But after the interview you were good enough to grant me, I persuaded myself to join it, – if for no other cause, then certainly out of my great regard for yourself.

One of my reasons for abstention, – and perhaps the strongest, – was that Mr. Tilak, Mrs. Besant, and the brothers Ali, whom I regard as among the most powerful leaders of public opinion, were not invited to the Conference. I still feel that it was a grave blunder not to have asked them, and I respectfully suggest that the blunder might be partially repaired if these leaders were invited to assist the Government by giving it the benefit of their advice at the Provincial Conferences which, I understand, are to follow. I venture to submit that no Government can afford to disregard leaders who represent large masses of the people, as these do, even though they may hold views fundamentally different. At the same time, it gives me pleasure to be able to say that the views of all parties were permitted to be freely expressed at the Committees of the Conference. For my own part, I purposely refrained from stating my views, either at the Committee on which I had the honour of serving – or at the Conference itself. I felt that I could best serve the objects of the Conference by simply tendering my support to the resolutions submitted to it, – and this I have done without any reservation. I hope to translate the spoken word into action as early as the Government can see its way to accept my offer, which I am submitting simultaneously herewith in a separate letter. I recognize that, in the hour of its danger, we must give, – as we have decided to give – ungrudging and unequivocal support to the Empire, of which we aspire, in the near future, to be partners in the same sense as the Dominions overseas. But it is the simple truth that our response is due to the expectation that our goal will be reached all the more speedily on that account – even as the performance of a duty automatically confers a corresponding right. The people are entitled to believe that the imminent reforms alluded to in your speech will embody the main, general principles of the Congress-League Scheme, and I am sure that it is this faith which has enabled many members of the Conference to tender to the Government their whole-hearted cooperation.

If I could make my countrymen retrace their steps, I would make them withdraw all the Congress resolutions, and not whisper 'Home Rule' or 'Responsible Government' during the pendency of the war. I would make India offer all her able-bodied sons as a sacrifice to the Empire at its critical moment; and I know that India by this very act would become the most favoured partner in the Empire and racial distinctions would become a thing of the past. But practically the whole of educated India has decided to take a less effective course, and it is no longer possible to say that educated India does not exercise any influence on the masses. I have been coming into most intimate touch with the riots ever since my return from South Africa to India, and I wish to assure you that the desire for Home Rule has widely penetrated them. I was present at the sessions of the last Congress, and I was party to the resolution that full Responsible Government should be granted to British India within a period to be fixed definitely by a Parliamentary Statute. I admit that it is a bold step to take, but I feel sure that nothing less than a definite vision of Home Rule – to be realized in the shortest possible time – will satisfy the Indian people. I know that there are many in India who consider no sacrifice too great in order to achieve the end; and they are wakeful enough to realize that they must be equally prepared to sacrifice themselves for the Empire in which they hope and desire to reach their final status. It follows, then, that we can but accelerate our journey towards the goal by silently and simply devoting ourselves, heart and soul, to the work of delivering the Empire from the threatening danger. It will be national suicide not to recognize this elementary truth. We must perceive that, if we serve to save the Empire, we have in that very act secured Home Rule. Whilst, therefore, it is clear to me that we should give to the Empire every available man for its defence, I fear that I cannot say the same thing about financial assistance. My intimate intercourse with the ryots [sic] convinces me that India has already donated to the Imperial Exchequer beyond her capacity. I know that, in making this statement, I am voicing the opinion of the vast majority of my countrymen.

The Conference means for me, and I believe for many of us, a definite step in the consecration of our lives to the common cause. But ours is a peculiar position. We are today outside the partnership. Ours is a consecration based on the hope of a better future. I should be untrue to you and to my country if I did not clearly and unequivocally tell you what that hope is. I do not bargain for its fulfilment. But you should know it. isappointment of the hope means disillusion.

There is one thing I may not omit. You have appealed to us to sink domestic differences. If the appeal involves the toleration of tyranny and wrongdoing on the part of officials, I am powerless to respond. I shall resist organized tyranny to the uttermost. The appeal must be to the officials that they do not ill-treat a single soul, and that they consult and respect popular opinion as never before. In Champaran, by resisting an age-long tyranny, I have shown the ultimate sovereignty of British justice. In Kaira, a population that was cursing the Government now feels that it, and not the Government, is the power when it is prepared to suffer for the truth it represents. It is, therefore, losing its bitterness and is saying to itself that the Government must be a Government for the people, for it tolerates orderly and respectful disobedience where injustice is felt. Thus, Champaran and Kaira affairs are my direct, definite, and special contribution to the war. Ask me to suspend my activities in that direction, and you ask me to suspend my life. If I could popularize the use of soul-force, which is but another name for love-force, in the place of brute force, I know that I could present you with an India that could defy the whole world to do its worst. In season and out of season, therefore, I shall discipline myself to express in my life this eternal law of suffering and present it for acceptance to those who care. And if I take part in any other activity, the motive is to show the matchless superiority of that law. Lastly, I would like you to ask His Majesty's Ministers to give definite assurances about Mahomedan States. I am sure you know that every Mahomedan is deeply interested in them. As a Hindu, I cannot be indifferent to their cause. Their sorrows must be our sorrows. In the most scrupulous regard for the right of these States, and for the Muslim sentiment as to places of worship and in your just and timely treatment of the Indian claim to Home Rule, lies the safety of the Empire.

I write this, because I love the English Nation, and I wish to evoke in every Indian the loyalty of the Englishman.

Gandhi

ON CIVIL DISOBEDIENCE:
CABLE TO E. S. MONTAGU,
LABURNUM ROAD, GAMDEVI
24 June 1919

To Right Hon'ble E. S. Montagu

I feel I ought to inform you that unless circumstances alter situation, I propose resuming civil disobedience early July. With me it is a creed. Whilst prosperity, just laws, just administration largely prevent criminal disobedience, I firmly believe nothing but civil disobedience with truth and non-injury as indispensable observances will ever replace criminal disobedience and onrush bolshevism. Governments whether alien or indigenous will sometimes grievously err even to extent flouting public opinion as has happened in case Rowlatt legislation. In such case discontent must either take form criminal disobedience and anarchical crime or may be and can be directed healthy channel by civil disobedience which is nothing but partial or total withdrawal of support by civil resisters from government in an orderly manner and without anger or ill will. I wish however that Rowlatt legislation could be withdrawn and committee of inquiry be appointed to investigate causes disturbances Punjab and administration martial law with power to revise sentences and that Kalinath Roy, editor *Tribune*, be released. I have already sent letter to Viceroy requesting above- mentioned relief.

Gandhi

ON RELIGIOUS LEADERS

There is a painful thing I am obliged to mention, and it is that our religious leaders, whose duty it is to enlighten people, have forgotten that duty. This is true, however much it may hurt us. Religious leaders have it in them to set an example to their followers by their conduct. Mere preaching will have no effect on those who assemble to listen to their discourses. Religious leaders, too, should follow the rule of swadeshi. They have plenty of time on hand. They should take to the spinning-wheel and spin and thus set an example to their followers. More than in the repetition of Rama as they tell the beads, in the music of the spinning-wheel will they hear the voice of the *atman* with a beauty all its own.

MESSAGE ON HIS ARREST
around 30 June 1919

As my arrest may come upon me unawares, I wish to leave the following as my message. I appeal to all my countrymen and countrywomen throughout India to observe absolute calmness and to refrain from violence to person and property in any shape or form. The greatest injury that can be done to me is deeds of violence after my arrest and for my sake. Those who love me will show their true affection only by becoming satyagrahis, i.e., believers in Truth and ahimsa (nonviolence) and self-suffering as the only means for securing redress of grievances. To the Government of India, I respectfully wish to submit that they will never establish peace in India by ignoring the causes of the present discontent. Satyagraha has not bred lawlessness and violence. It is a vital force and it has certainly hastened the crisis that was inevitable. But it has also acted as a restraining force of the first magnitude. Government as well as the people should recognize this fact and feel thankful for it. Without the purifying and soothing effect of satyagraha, violence would have been infinitely greater, for mutual retaliation would have produced nothing but chaos. Mahomedans are deeply resentful of what they believe to be England's attitude towards the question of Turkey, Palestine and Mecca Sharif. The people are deeply distrustful of England's attitude towards the forthcoming Reforms and they want repeal of the Rowlatt legislation.

CHAPTER 3

The Middle Period

ON BLIND FAITH

It is the khadi cause that Shri Harjivan Kotak is serving on behalf of the Charkha Sangh in Srinagar, the capital of Kashmir. But the heart of a khadi worker certainly melts at the sight of misery wherever he sees it. Hence, when the pilgrims to Amarnath suffered hardships due to excessive rain, he sent me a telegram. When I asked for details, I received the following reply:

'What a contrast between Amarnath and lorries! There was a time when pilgrims travelled on foot from Kanyakumari to Kashmir and then, after suffering many hardships, ascended Amarnath. Even in those days, there was danger to life. We have no figures about the number of people who in those days lost their dear lives while in quest of religious merit, as there were no figures about other things.'

ON THE SPINNING WHEEL

This [Uttukuli] is a heavy production centre for hand-spinning and weaving. I have half picked up this work here. There are about a thousand spinners. I have gone about the villages and met many of them in their own little cottages. Every day that passes makes me marvel the more as to how you discovered the spinning-wheel. I am very much tempted to ask if you could not kindly tell in the pages of Young India when and how exactly you re-discovered the wheel. It is so little and so big at the same time. It reminds me of the rain drops – each so tiny by itself but together 'the mighty ocean'. Nothing is more wrong than to think that you have asked India to spin and that India has begun to spin driven to do so by you. The truth is rather that the millions in the villages have driven you to it – to be their agent for disposing of all their yarn. I am daily watching crowds of old women and girls coming with their yarn. They come with smiling faces, their precious yarn clutched to their hearts. And khadi is retouching slowly into life just those vital parts of our national being that have been touched almost into death by this most soulless of exploitations. I realize now as never before the truth of your words when you said that the world would some day accept khadi as the noblest of your works. He is right when he says that the toiling, starving millions drove me to it. It was in London in 1909 that I discovered the wheel. I had gone there leading a deputation from South Africa. It was then that I came in close touch with many earnest Indians – students and others. We had many long conversations about the condition of India and I saw as in a flash that without the spinning-wheel there was no swaraj. I knew at once that everyone had to spin.

ON THE HINDU–MUSLIM FIGHT
IN GODRHA

On Wednesday, I received a postcard from Godhra informing me that, in the fighting that took place there between Hindus and Muslims on the occasion of the Paryushan festival, Shri Wamanrao Mukadam, Shri Purushottamdas Shah and some other Hindus have been seriously injured. Today, that is, on Thursday, at the time of writing this, I received a telegram informing me of Shri Purushottamdas's death. I am aware of my inability to do anything besides expressing my sympathy to the bereaved family and I am sorry on this account. Hence I write nothing these days on this subject near my heart. I do not believe I have the right to say anything on it. I have come to the conclusion that the medicine I have is wanted by neither side. I have no other medicine with me except non-violence and love. At present it is not possible for me to explain the efficacy of this medicine to anyone. Hence I believe and am aware that silence is proper for me. My silence is my sole contribution to the efforts for unity. But this silence does not mean indifference. As I believe in prayer, I ceaselessly pray to God to give wisdom to both the communities and ordain that unity of hearts be established among them. If this prayer is sincere, I am bound sooner or later to find some means of ending this enmity.

LETTER TO MOTILAL NEHRU
30 September 1928

Dear Motilalji,

Mahadev gave me your message. But as there was nothing definite to say and as I have been overwhelmed with work in connection with the Ashram, I did not write to you before now. Mahadev tells me that you want me to attend the All-India Congress Committee's meeting. What shall I do there? What can I do? I know that that part of the national work is also useful, but my heart has gone out of it and I become more and more inclined to give my time to what is concisely understood as constructive work. I do not mention khadi alone, because I am giving such attention as I can to other items of constructive work not even mentioned in the Congress programme. And I see that everywhere strength of mind has got to be evoked and to the extent that it is, the power of resistance is developed. Lucknow seems evidently to have left the masses untouched.

Today riots are going on in Gujarat which never before knew Hindu-Muslim rioting. News has just arrived that a brave Ashram lad was nearly done to death yesterday. Whilst he was in a press building, the goondas broke into that building, indiscriminately assaulted every-one who was in it and then set fire to it. A noted Vakil of Godhra was fatally wounded and Waman Rao who is a member of the Bombay Council and whom you know was seriously assaulted. Every day some fresh rioting news comes from some place or other. I know that in spite of all this, the constitution-building work must be done. I only want to tell you that these riots largely unfit me for such work. Indeed, I am contemplating absence even from the Congress if you could permit me to remain away. There is a double reason: the prevailing atmosphere and the decision of the Calcutta Committee to copy the Madras type of Exhibition. The Council of the All-India Spinners' Association has decided to abstain from being represented at that Exhibition. Much though I feel the error in using Madras Exhibition as a type, I do not want to criticize it in the public. If I go to Calcutta, my presence will either embarrass the Committee or my silence will embarrass me. I have now given you what is today oppressing my mind. You will now decide firstly, whether you want me for the All-India Congress Committee in Calcutta and secondly, whether you want me to attend the Congress in December. You and Vithalbhai worked wonders in Simla.

Yours sincerely,

Gandhi

TELEGRAM TO ANNIE BESANT
5 October 1928

Dr Besant

Your wire. Am convinced it will be disastrous if Nehru Constitution breaks down for want country's support which can be given without prejudice to attempts made realize independence goal. Whilst I agree that maximum agreement among parties not always essential we should strive for it in matters like this where no national interest is compromised.

Gandhi

ON GOD – FROM A SPEECH
RECORDED IN KINGSLEY HALL
around December 1928

I permit myself to state why I believe. I am prompted to do so because of the knowledge that there are young men who are interested in my views and doings. There is an indefinable mysterious Power that pervades everything. I feel It, though I do not see It. It is this unseen Power which makes Itself felt and yet defies all proof, because It is so unlike all that I perceive through my senses. It transcends the senses. But it is possible to reason out the existence of God to a limited extent. Even in ordinary affairs we know that people do not know, who rules or why and how he rules. And yet they know that there is a power that certainly rules. In my tour last year in Mysore I met many poor villagers and I found upon inquiry that they did not know who ruled Mysore. They simply said some god ruled it. If the knowledge of these poor people was so limited about their ruler, I, who am infinitely lesser than God than they than their ruler, need not be surprised if I do not realize the presence of God, the King of kings.

Nevertheless I do feel as the poor villagers felt about Mysore that there is orderliness in the Universe, there is an unalterable Law governing everything and every being that exists or lives. It is not a blind law; for no blind law can govern the conduct of living beings and, thanks to the marvellous researches of Sir J. C. Bose, it can now be proved that even matter is life. That Law then which governs all life is God. Law and the Law-giver are one. I may not deny the Law or the Law-giver, because I know so little about It or Him. Even as my denial or ignorance of the existence of an earthly power will avail me nothing, so will not my denial of God and His Law liberate me from its operation; whereas humble and mute acceptance of divine authority makes life's journey easier even as the acceptance of earthly rule makes life under it easier.

I do dimly perceive that whilst everything around me is ever changing, ever dying, there is underlying all that change a living Power that is changeless, that holds all together, that creates, dissolves and recreates. That informing Power or Spirit is God. And since nothing else I see merely through the senses can or will persist, He alone is.

And is this Power benevolent or malevolent? I see It as purely benevolent. For I can see that in the midst of death life persists, in the midst of untruth, truth persists, in the midst of darkness light persists. Hence I gather that God is Life, Truth, Light. He is Love. He is the supreme Good. But he is no God who merely satisfies the intellect if He ever does. God to be God must rule the heart and transform it. He must express Himself in every smallest act of His votary. This can only be done through a definite realization more real than the five senses can ever produce. Sense perceptions can be, often are, false and deceptive, however real they may appear to us. Where there is realization outside the senses it is infallible. It is proved not by extraneous evidence but in the transformed conduct and character of those who have felt the real presence of God within. Such testimony is to be found in the experiences of an unbroken line of prophets and sages in all countries and climes. To reject this evidence is to deny oneself. This realization is preceded by an immovable faith. He who would in his own person test the fact of God's presence can do so by a living faith. And since faith itself cannot be proved by extraneous evidence, the safest course is to believe in the moral government of the world and therefore in the supremacy of the moral law, the law of truth and love. Exercise of faith will be the safest where there is a clear determination summarily to reject all that is contrary to Truth and Love. Faith transcends reason. All I can advise is not to attempt the impossible. I cannot account for the existence of evil by any rational method.

To want to do so is to be coequal with God. I am therefore humble enough to recognize evil as such. And I call God long-suffering and patient precisely because He permits evil in the world. I know that He has no evil in Him, and yet if there is evil, He is the author of it and yet untouched by it.

I know too that I shall never know God if I do not wrestle with and against evil even at the cost of life itself. I am fortified in the belief by my own humble and limited experience. The purer I try to become, the nearer I feel to be to God. How much more should I be, when my faith is not a mere apology as it is today but has become as immovable as the Himalayas and as white and bright as the snows on their peaks? Meanwhile I invite the correspondent to pray with Newman who sang from experience:

> Lead, kindly Light, amid the encircling gloom,
> Lead Thou me on; The night is dark and I am far
>   from home,
> Lead Thou me on; Keep Thou my feet,
> I do not ask to see The distant scene; one step's
>   enough for me.

LETTER ON RAMA AND ANGER TO AVADHESH DUTT AVASTHI
7 May 1935

Chi. Avadhesh

Tulsidas himself has said that the name of Rama is greater than Rama, meaning that Rama, who transcends the body, is formless and nameless and is greater than Rama in body. Rama was certainly the son of Dasharatha and the husband of Sita, but He is also the Purushottama of our imagination because the Unmanifest is not different from the Manifest. Everything is a manifestation of the Unmanifest. I don't insist on the name Rama, it might be Omkar or Krishna, or Ishwar.

I do get angry, but I feel angry with myself for it. Full conquest of anger is possible only through self-realization. We should love even those who have the worst opinion of us. This is ahimsa, the rest is only ignorance.

Blessings from

Bapu

LETTER TO AVADHESH DUTT AVASTHI
15 May 1935

Chi. Avadhesh

May our nation become and remain the greatest in respect of all moral values. Man's self-respect lies in uplifting himself and in doing this not fearing even death. Why is anger necessary for protecting our self-respect and fighting wickedness? If I am told to rub my nose on the ground I may not be angry and yet refuse to comply and bear cheerfully whatever punishment is vouchsafed for my disobedience. Dharma is that which uplifts the soul. We shall think that God is a name for Truth, God is identical with truth.

Blessings from Bapu

LETTER TO MANUBEHN MASHRUWALA
17 September 1938

Chi. Manudi,

Consider yourself fortunate that you have arrived when I am observing silence. That silence is for the whole country. You have the benefit of being a witness to it. The silence is not an expression of diminished love. Love does not care for words uttered by the tongue. I will certainly write to you when you go to Bombay. You should write, too.

Blessings from Bapu

FEDERATION HARIJAN
1 October 1938

A well-known correspondent tells me that in London the common talk is that Gandhi counts for everything and it does not matter what the Congress or Congressmen may say or do. The critics embellish the statement by saying that there is a wide difference of opinion between Pandit Jawaharlal Nehru and myself, and that while he will not touch Federation with a pair of tongs, I am prepared to submit to it if some trifles are conceded. I have paraphrased in my own words a longish letter giving details which I may not share with the readers at least at the present juncture.

Evidently my critics know more of me than I seem to know myself. For instance I know how little I count among Congressmen; the critics know how much I count among them. Whatever influence I still possess among Congressmen is solely due to my constant appeal to reason and never to authority. But if I had the influence the critics attribute to me, I make bold to say that India would have gained her independence long ago and there would be no repression that is going on unchecked in some of the States. I know the art of winning independence and stopping the frightfulness of which one reads in the papers. If I had my way with the Congressmen, there would be no corruption, no untruth and no violence amongst them. If I had my way with them, they would all be enthusiastic khaddarites and there would be no surplus khadi in the A.I.S.A. bhandars.

But I am going astray. I had intended to write about Federation. In the first place, in all my talks, which have been very few, I have made it clear that I represent nobody and that I have not even aired my views to any Congressman. I have also made it clear that what the Congress says and does is of consequence, whatever I may say is of no value unless it represents the Congress view. As a matter of fact, too, I have said that the Congress will never have Federation forced upon it, and that there was no hope of peace in India till there was independence in virtue of a constitution framed by a duly convened Constituent Assembly. I have also made it clear that so far as Pandit Jawaharlal Nehru and I are concerned, though we may talk in different language, we are one in most things that matter to India. On the question of Federation there never has been any difference of opinion between us. And I have made a rule for myself that so far as the Congress in concerned, if there is an unbridgeable gulf between him and me his view should prevail. And this for the very good reason that I am not in the Congress and he is in the centre of it, and very much in touch with everything relating to the Congress.

INTERVIEW BY PRESTON GROVER,
Wardha, 10 June 1942

Q. *There has been a great deal of questioning in America and India to as to the nature of your activities during the balance of the War. I should like to know what it will be like.*

A. But can you tell me when the War will end?

Q. *There is a good deal of speculation that you are planning some new movement. What is the nature of it?*

A. It depends on the response made by the Government and the people. I am trying to find out public opinion here and also the reaction on the world outside.

Q. *When you speak of the response, you mean response to your new proposal?*

A. Oh yes, I mean response to the proposal that the British Government in India should end today. Are you startled?

Q. *I am not. You have been asking for it and working for it.*

A. That's right. I have been working for it for years. But now it has taken definite shape and I say that the British power in India should go today for the world peace, for China, for Russia and for the Allied cause. I shall explain to you how it advances the Allied cause. Complete independence frees India's energies, frees her to make her contribution to the world crisis. Today the Allies are carrying the burden of a huge corpse – a huge nation lying prostrate at the feet of Britain, I would even say at the feet of the Allies. For America is the predominant partner, financing the war, giving her mechanical ability and her resources which are inexhaustible. America is thus a partner in the guilt.

Q. *Do you see a situation when after full independence is granted American and Allied troops can operate from India?*

A. I do. It will be only then that you will see real coop-eration. Otherwise all the effort you put up may fail. Just now Britain is having India's resources because India is her possession. Tomorrow whatever the help, it will be real help from a *free* India.

Q. *You think India in control interferes with Allied action to meet Japan's aggression?*

A. It does.

Q. *When I mentioned Allied troops operating I wanted to know whether you contemplated complete shifting of the present troops from India?*

A. Not necessarily.

Q. *It is on this that there is a lot of misconception.*

A. You have to study all I am writing. I have discussed

the whole question in the current issue of *Harijan*.
I do not want them to go, on condition that India
becomes entirely free. I cannot then insist on their
withdrawal, because I want to resist with all my
might the charge of inviting Japan to India.

*Q. But suppose your proposal is rejected, what will be your
next move?*

A. It will be a move which will be felt by the whole
world. It may not interfere with the movement
of British troops, but it is sure to engage British
attention. It would be wrong of them to reject my
proposal and say India should remain a slave in order
that Britain may win or be able to defend China. I
cannot accept that degrading position. India free and
independent will play a prominent part in defending
China. Today I do not think she is rendering any real
help to China. We have followed the non-embarrassment policy so far. We will follow it even now. But
we cannot allow the British Government to exploit
it in order to strengthen the stranglehold on India.
And today it amounts to that. The way, for instance,
in which thousands are being asked to vacate their
homes with nowhere to go to, no land to cultivate,
no resources to fall back upon, is the reward of our
non-embarrassment. This should be impossible in
any free country. I cannot tolerate India submitting
to this kind of treatment. It means greater degradation and servility, and when a whole nation accepts

servility it means good-bye for ever to freedom.

Q. *All you want is the civil grip relaxed. You won't then hinder military activity?*

A. I do not know. I want unadulterated independence. If the military activity serves but to strengthen the stranglehold, I must resist that too. I am no philanthropist to go on helping at the expense of my freedom. And what I want you to see is that a corpse cannot give any help to a living body. The Allies have no moral cause for which they are fighting, so long as they are carrying this double sin on their shoulders, the sin of India's subjection and the subjection of the Negroes and African races. Mr. Grover did not seriously press the point.

Q. *You don't expect any assistance from America in persuading Britain to relinquish her hold on India.*

A. I do indeed.

Q. *With any possibility of success?*

A. There is every possibility, I should think. I have every right to expect America to throw her full weight on the side of justice, if she is convinced of the justice of the Indian cause.

Q. *You don't think the American Government is committed to the British remaining in India?*

A. I hope not. But British diplomacy is so clever that

America, even though it may not be committed, and in spite of the desire of President Roosevelt and the people to help India, it may not succeed. British propaganda is so well organized in America against the Indian cause that the few friends India has there have no chance of being effectively heard. And the political system is so rigid that public opinion does not affect the administration.

Q. *It may, slowly.*

A. Slowly? I have waited long, and I can wait no longer. It is a terrible tragedy that 40 crores of people should have no say in this war. If we have the freedom to play our part we can arrest the march of Japan and save China.

Q. *What specific things would be done by India to save China, if India is declared independent?*

A. Great things, I can say at once, though I may not be able to specify them today. For I do not know what government we shall have. We have various political organizations here which I expect would be able to work out a proper national solution. Just now they are not solid parties, they are often acted upon by the British power, they look up to it and its frown or favour means much to them. The whole atmosphere is corrupt and rotten. Who can foresee the possibilities of a corpse coming to life? At present India is a dead weight to the Allies.

Q. By dead weight you mean a menace to Britain and to American interests here?

A. I do. It is a menace in that you never know what sullen India will do at a given moment.

Q. No, but I want to make myself sure that if genuine pressure was brought to bear on Britain by America, there would be solid support from yourself?

A. Myself? I do not count – with the weight of 73 years on my shoulders. But you get the co-operation – whatever it can give willingly – of a free and mighty nation. My co-operation is of course there. I exercise what influence I can by my writings from week to week. But India's is an infinitely greater influence. Today because of widespread discontent there is not that active hostility to Japanese advance. The moment we are free, we are transformed into a nation prizing its liberty and defending it with all its might and therefore helping the Allied cause.

Q. May I concretely ask – will the difference be the difference that there is between what Burma did and what, say, Russia is doing?

A. You might put it that way. They might have given Burma independence after separating it from India. But they did nothing of the kind. They stuck to the same old policy of exploiting her. There was little co-operation from Burmans; on the contrary there was hostility or inertia. They fought neither for their own cause nor for the Allied cause. Now take a possible contingency. If the Japanese compel the Allies to retire from India to a safer base, I cannot say *today* that the whole of India will be up in arms against the Japanese. I have a fear that they may degrade themselves as some Burmans did. I want India to oppose Japan to a man. If India was free she would do it, it would be a new experience to her, in twenty-four hours her mind would be changed. All parties would then act as one man. If this live independence is declared today I have no doubt India becomes a powerful ally. I can only say that as soon as the vicious influence of the third party is withdrawn, the parties will be face to face with reality and close up ranks. Ten to one my conviction is that the communal quarrels will disappear as soon as the British power that keeps us apart disappears.

Q. Would not Dominion Status declared today do equally well?

A. No good. We will have no half measures, no tinkering with independence. It is not independence that they will give to this party or that party, but to an indefinable India. It was wrong, I say, to possess India. The wrong should be righted by leaving India to herself. I say that if the war is to be decisively won, India must be freed to play her part today. I find no flaw in my position. I have arrived at it after considerable debating within myself; I am doing nothing in hurry or anger. There is not the slightest room in me for accommodating the Japanese. No, I am sure that India's independence is not only essential for India, but for China and the Allied cause.

Q. *What are the exact steps by which you will save China?*

A. The whole of India's mind would be turned away from Japan. Today it is not. C. R. knows it, and it worries him as it should worry any sane patriot. It worried me no less, but it drives me to a contrary conclusion. India lying at the feet of Great Britain may mean China lying at the feet of Japan. I cannot help using this language. I feel it. You may think it startling and big. But why should it be startling? Think of 400 million people hungering for freedom. They want to be left alone. They are not savages. They have an ancient culture, ancient civilization, such variety and richness of languages. Britain should be ashamed of holding these people as slaves.

You may say: 'You deserve it!' If you do, I will simply say it is not right for any nation to hold another in bondage. I say even if a nation should want to be in bondage it should be derogatory to one's dignity to keep it in bondage. But you have your own difficulties. You have yet to abolish slavery!

Q. *In the United States, you mean?*

A. Yes, your racial discrimination, your lynch law and so on. But you don't want me to remind you of these things.

CHAPTER 4

Victory

SPEECH AT A PRAYER MEETING
IN NEW DELHI
9 July 1947

Brothers and sisters,

You will ask me why I went to see the Viceroy today. Freedom is not yet ours. There is only hostility. They stop the trams as they like, they stab and loot. Freedom is like the sun but it does not seem to me that it is coming. The Viceroy calls me his friend. How can I be a friend of his? I am a friend of the sweepers, of the poor.

The writer of the letter I spoke of yesterday reminds me that in 1940 I had said that I found violence in the air. He asks if I found violence in the air then, what do I find now? He has the right to ask. It cannot be said that things are going well in India. People are stopping trains, indulging in arson and plunder and stabbings. This is anarchy. People embezzle funds and adopt improper methods to make money. Others quietly part with money. There is untruth, violence, hatred and distrust in the air.

Against this background comes the declaration of June 3. Hindus, Muslims and Sikhs have agreed to see India dismembered. Then came reports in newspapers of thefts, looting, arson and murders. The correspondent sarcastically asks me if this is my idea of love. He says I have been a votary of truth and asks where that truth is now. Now the only question is, who is higher and who is lower? Where is the tolerance I have been talking about? If it is not there, who is responsible for it? Is it the Viceroy or is it someone else?

My answer is that it is true that there is a stench everywhere. I say I am responsible for it. For thirty years I have been telling the country to follow truth and non-violence. If my advice had been heeded, the result would have been different. You judge the tree by the fruit. If the English go, does it mean that law and order should also go with them? Even people who talked that language of satyagraha had harboured thoughts of violence and intended at the very first opportunity to take to arms. The swaraj I had dreamed of is still a long way away. I do not wish to be a witness to this internecine strife. I do not wish to shed tears over what has happened in Multan, Rawalpindi, Garhmukteshwar, Bihar and Bengal, for I am a soldier. Nor do I wish to die. Neither the Hindus, nor the Muslims, nor the Sikhs can ensure their survival through the madness that has overtaken them. Money can be earned by the sword but no merit. The only way is for us even now to take to the path of non-violence. Therein alone lies our good and that of the world. Humanity demands that the British should bring about reconciliation between the two parties, between the two armies. I hope that the days that are left will be enough to achieve this. Then there is the question of the States. Fifteenth of August is the last day. There is still time. If reconciliation cannot be effected before that date, then I fear it will be too late. The British are stronger than we. They have immense military strength. Those who imagine that the British are finished as a military power are mistaken.

I have been asked: 'Whereas in Pakistan Mr. Jinnah has been made Governor-General, here in India it is the

Viceroy who has been made Governor-General. Why should this be so? The battle for India's freedom was fought by the Congress. The Muslim League has had no part in it. Whenever the Congress resorted to civil disobedience or satyagraha, the League refused to co-operate. Even so the Congress cannot get an Indian as Governor-General. This is not just. This will mean that we shall be safe only if we kowtow to the British or we shall die.' I shall say that under the scheme that will come into effect on August 15, it does not matter whether the Governor-General is an Englishman, a Frenchman or a Dutchman, whether he is a brownskinned Indian or a White or a Negro. If I had my way a Harijan girl would be the Governor-General. So if Lord Mountbatten becomes the Governor-General he will still be a servant of India. You will say this is the kind of talk to pacify children. Mountbatten, who is a scion of a Royal family, will not be anybody's servant. But I am not deceiving you. I do not expect any reward from Lord Mountbatten. So long I have been fighting against him. Maybe you will say that the Congress leaders have been deceived by him. Do you mean to say that Jawaharlal, Sardar and Rajaji are so softbrained as to be taken in? True, as I have been saying what I had wanted has not come to pass. But Mountbatten will be Governor-General because we want him. If we did not want him he would not hold that office. But Mr. Jinnah may have chosen to be Governor-General in order to show off. We should not be jealous and we should not be angry. He wants to show to the world what Islam is. Let us see whether he makes of himself a master or a servant. If even a single Sindhi flees, then the responsibility for it will rest on the Governor-General of Pakistan. He will have to be just to all, like Abubaker or Omar, or Ali. I do not say they were all non-violent. But I have in mind their bravery and their chivalry. I understand from the newspapers that originally the idea had been for India and Pakistan to have one Governor-General in common. But Mr. Jinnah later went back on his word. Who was then to prevent him from becoming the Governor-General of Pakistan? In my view he did not do the right thing. When he had once agreed he should have accepted Lord Mountbatten as Governor-General and later if something had gone wrong he could have removed him. Now Islam is to be tested through Mr. Jinnah. He is assuming the Governor-Generalship of Pakistan with the whole world as witness.

The world will now wait to see what special virtues Pakistan displays under him. The Congress has always been fighting against the British. Jawaharlal is a simple-hearted man. But the Sardar is a fighter. He used to quarrel with me because I trusted the British. When he himself has been caught up in their wiles, what can you or I hope to do? When he agrees that the Viceroy should be the first Governor-General of India, why should we object? We shall see whether he will serve India as Governor-General or betray her. It will be a new experience. There is wisdom in this and we have nothing to lose. After all we accepted Dominion Status on the advice of the Viceroy. He is an Admiral and a great warrior. Let us have him and if he does not come up to our expectations we can always fight with him. When I went to see the Viceroy he confided in me that the young man to whom Princess Elizabeth had been betrothed was like a son to him and he hoped that I would write a few words of blessings to him. So when the Viceroy's daughter came to see me two days ago I gave her a letter of congratulation addressed to the couple. She is such a sweet girl. At the prayer I offered her a chair but she declined the offer and sat down with us on the duree. And today I learnt from Rajkumari Amrit Kaur that the young Princess who has got engaged to be married will be the future queen of England because the king has no son. The Viceroy too has no son. Anyway if the Viceroy had been a bad man I wouldn't have been so free with my blessings. I do not consider him a bad man. If Jawaharlal or Sardar Patel had become Governor-General in his place it would have been a dangerous thing. Besides, the Governor-General wields no effective power. He will have to act on the advice of Jawaharlal and his cabinet. He will only be a figurehead.

But we have got into the way of thinking that Lord Mountbatten has great status and the English are capable only of devilry. Lord Mountbatten therefore will have to prove his honesty and love of justice and I am sure that he has come to India to do only justice.

ON INDIA AND PAKISTAN

My creed is nonviolence.

I have never waged war, nor should anyone else do so. How can we achieve anything by fighting? What I said was that if Pakistan was committing mistakes or if India was committing mistakes, with both the countries having their own independent Governments, how was it possible for one Government to secure justice from the other? It would be different if the two Governments worked in co-operation. Let them have an arbitrator if they cannot work together. If even that cannot be done, then we shall helplessly be dragged into war. Does this imply advocating war? I want to tell both India and Pakistan that they must come to a mutual settlement or accept an arbitrator. But if the Pakistanis insist on taking India by force, then, as I said yesterday, India would have no alternative except to fight. If I am given the charge of the Government I would follow a different path, because I have no military and police force under me. But I am the only one to follow that path. Who would support me? Your Government will do what is expected of it when the time comes. I would continue to chant only one refrain. But, if people do not respect non-violence, what can I do?

FROM A SPEECH AT A PRAYER MEETING
7 October 1947

Today we have got power in our hands. We have got our own ministers. Our Prime Minister is Jawaharlal. He is a true jewel and he has served his people well. Then there is the Sardar and there are others too. Is it that we do not like them? Today it is said Jawaharlal is no good. It is said he is not a good Hindu. People want a person who will follow their dictates, who will not support the Muslims and will drive them out. I must admit that Jawaharlal cannot do so. Nor can I do so. I consider myself a sanatani Hindu. But I am not that sanatani who would not let anyone except the Hindus live in India. Whatever the religion one may follow, one belongs to India if one is loyal to the country, and is as much entitled to live in India as I am. It makes no difference if one belongs to the minority community. That is what religion teaches me. Right from my childhood I have been taught that in *Ramarajya* or the Kingdom of God no person can be unworthy just because he follows a different religion. You must realize that I am such a Hindu. I have no power in my hands and I am not a minister. Jawaharlal is a minister and you can remove him if you want. Then there is the Sardar. Do you know who he is? He is the Sardar from Bardoli. Do you listen to him? He also has many Muslim friends. His friend Imam Saheb was the Congress leader in Gujarat and he is dead. Imam Saheb's son-in-law is at Ahemedabad and I think he is the chief of the District Congress. He is a very goodhearted man. I know him very well. He married

Imam Saheb's daughter. It is the same Imam Saheb who came away with his wife from South Africa, leaving his business there, and stayed with me. He is dead and his grown-up daughter is left behind. Should I discard her and tell her that I have nothing to do with her because she is a Muslim? She is a Muslim no doubt, but I can say that she is a good-hearted girl. She does not know that she might have to leave. If the Sardar lets her go, where is she going to stay? Let us not take the law into our own hands. Law may be made by the Sardar or Jawaharlal, but they cannot first issue ordinances and then leave the matter to the public. Today we cannot have such ministers. Granted that that was done during the days of the British. But does it mean that we should do so even now? Shall we invite the same criticism about us which we used to fling at the British? We will not tolerate it. That is all I want to say.

CHAPTER 5

The End

This is the final entry in Mr Gandhi's *Collected Works* before his tragic assassination.

NEW DELHI, 12 JANUARY 1948
reported in *The Bombay Chronicle*
13 January 1948

I am sure all of you have read the Press statement of Mr. Ghulam Mohammad, Finance Minister of Pakistan, on the payment of cash balances to the Pakistan Government. The Finance Minister of Pakistan has had a varied career of responsibility as a civil servant – Finance Minister of Hyderabad State, and a participant in 'big business'. One would not normally expect in his statements the defects of *suppressio veri* and *suggestio falsi*. But I regret to observe that not only does his statement abound in these, but in his utter desperation at seeing his financial anticipations wrecked by the actions of his own Government in regard to Kashmir, he has cast discretion and judgment to the winds and descended down to the familiar arts of a bully and a blackmailer.

I use these epithets deliberately, for to anyone reading his statement dispassionately it would be obvious that he has tried to browbeat the Reserve Bank of India into submission by a liberal use of threats and insinuations, has charged the Government of India with bad faith in the hope that the charge would gain for him his coveted ransom, and has tried to invoke the assistance of international opinion in the expectation that the threatened exposure before the world would make the Government of India bend in its attitude on this subject. I quite concede that the desperate situation in which he finds himself calls for rather drastic remedies but we are entitled to expect of him a balanced approach to this problem rather than these filibustering tactics, the failure of which is as certain as daylight. Further, in his overzeal to achieve his object by all manner of means, the Pakistan Finance Minister has, I would presently show, paid little attention to truth and shown little regard for facts.

Let us first deal with his statement that 'none of us had the slightest indication that the Kashmir problem would be dragged in', his accusation of bad faith and similar other statements of an accusatory nature. To deal with these I would give in brief a resume of the course of negotiations. The series of meetings held between the representatives of the Pakistan and the Indian Governments in the last week of November were intended to iron out all our differences including the question of Kashmir. The discussions held were not confined to mere partition issues, but covered Kashmir, refugees and other important evacuation matters as well. On the 26th November talks on Kashmir were held in an atmosphere of hope, goodwill and cordiality, and were continued simultaneously with the discussions of financial and other questions on subsequent days. On the 27th November, informal and provisional agreement was reached on the two issues of division of cash balances, and the sharing of the uncovered debt. The Pakistan representatives were in some haste and tried to hustle us into agreeing to announce these agreements. We resisted it. Indeed, on the 27th evening, I issued a statement to the Press asking them not to speculate on the nature of the talks, but to wait until an authoritative statement was issued after the talks had concluded.

Here is what I said then: 'All-out efforts are being made for a settlement on all outstanding matters, but any speculations on the nature of the talks would do more harm than good. All that I can say at present is that discussions are being held and the Prime Minister and the Finance Minister of the Pakistan Government are staying on till Saturday. A detailed statement will be issued when the talks are concluded. Till then reports about any settlement on any individual item or issue between the two Governments must be regarded as premature and lacking authority.'

The next morning my statement which was read at a meeting at Government House at which both the Prime Minister and the Finance Minister of Pakistan were present, that we would not regard the settlement of these issues as final unless agreement had been reached on all outstanding issues. I made it quite clear then that we would not agree to any payment until the Kashmir affair was settled. Accordingly, no announcement of the agreement was made. In the meantime, Pakistan representatives postponed their departure, and talks on Kashmir and other matters were continued with rather varying results on different issues. Working in this somewhat improved atmosphere, we reached a settlement on all other out-standing issues relating to partition, and the informal agreement was reported to the Partition Council at its meeting on the 1st December, though they were to be reduced to writing later. This was completed on the 2nd December, but it was agreed even then not to make an announcement on the subject until after the Lahore discussions on Kashmir and other outstanding issues had been, as was then hoped, successfully concluded.

The position was further confirmed by the submission made on the 3rd December by both the parties before the Arbitral Tribunal that the prospects of all the references being settled were very good, that a further meeting was to be held on the 8th and 9th at Lahore and the situation would then be clearer. The discussions were resumed at Lahore on the 8th and 9th December. But in the meantime, it was found that feverish attempts were being made by the Pakistan Government to secure the payment of Rs. 55 crores which it had been agreed to allocate to Pakistan out of the cash balances. We resisted these attempts. Nevertheless, evidently in an attempt to isolate the issue and force our hands contrary to the understanding reached, the Pakistan High Commissioner on the 7th December gave a Press interview announcing the agreement reached on the financial issues. When, however, we stuck to our previous position and reiterated it during the Lahore discussion, though in deference to Pakistan's insistence on the announcement of the agreement on financial issues we agreed to make a short statement on the 9th December in the Legislature, which was then sitting in Delhi, the

Pakistan Finance Minister showed also such indecent haste in rushing to the Press in this matter that he actually gave an interview on the subject on the 7th December itself. Pakistan's game was by then quite clear.

Armed with this understanding on the question of public announcement by us of the agreement on financial issues, their attitude on the Kashmir stiffened and the prospect of agreement which seemed so near at Delhi receded. I then felt it necessary in my statement to the Assembly on 9th December to make it quite clear that the implementation of this agreement was to be as far as possible simultaneous with the settlement of the Kashmir issue. The Pakistan Government did not take any exception to this statement at the time. In the subsequent detailed statement which I made on the 12th in the presence of the Pakistan High Commissioner, I again repeated that the successful implementation of this agreement depended on the continuation of goodwill, spirit of accommodation and conciliation on the other vital issues. Quite obviously Kashmir was one of such issues. Pakistan still made no protest. To all approaches for payment of the Rs. 55 crores, we returned a negative answer. Then came the final talks on the Kashmir issue on the 22nd December. It was then for the first time during these discussions that the Pakistan Prime Minister took exception to our stand that the financial and Kashmir issues stood together as regards implementation and asked for immediate implementation of the payment of Rs. 55 crores. We made it clear to him then and subsequently in our telegram dated the 30th December that we stood by the agreement but that in view of the hostile attitude of the Pakistan Government in regard to Kashmir the payment of the amount would have to be postponed in accordance with our stand throughout the negotiations.

Thus it is our case that far from our having done anything unfair to Pakistan or in breach of any agreement, it is the Pakistan representatives who were all the time trying to soft-pedal the Kashmir issue in order to secure concessions from us on the financial issues and to manoeuvre us into making an isolated public announcement on the subject without reference to other vital issues between the two Governments. We consistently and successfully resisted this despite attempts by the Pakistan High Commissioner and Finance Minister to force our hands. Far from there being bad faith on our part, we genuinely and sincerely meant this settlement as part of an overall settlement which would have been conducive to the maintenance of friendly and peaceful relations between the two sister Dominions.

It is also our claim that in agreeing to these terms of the financial settlement, we were actuated by generous sentiments towards Pakistan and a sincere desire, as I made clear in the Partition Council, 'to see Pakistan grow into a prosperous neighbour'. We hoped that Pakistan would recip-rocate on other issues which unfortunately still divided us. That the financial settlement was attractive to Pakistan and would be a great asset to Pakistan's economy is clear from the statements issued by the Pakistan High Commissioner and Sir Archibald Rowlands (former Finance Member of Viceroy's Council). It is, therefore, quite plain that having secured terms which were essential to hold Pakistan's finances together, the Pakistan Government failed in their obligation to respond to India's gesture on other issues.

I would also point out that the Government of India took a more comprehensive view of our obligation to the securing of a just and peaceful settlement than the Pakistan Government. We realized throughout that neighbourly relations between ourselves and Pakistan could be restored and maintained only if the spirit of amity, tolerance and goodwill pervaded throughout the entire field of controversy; the Pakistan Government obviously intended to take undue advantage of our generous attitude and exhibit these virtues in a narrow, restricted and selfish sphere. The need for a comprehensive view was and still is quite clear. Apart from other factors, India has taken over the entire debt of undivided India and depends on Pakistan's bona fides and goodwill to make equated payment by easy and long-term instalments of its debt to India after a four-year moratorium period. We cannot, therefore, afford to let conflicts endanger our credit and security and throw into the melting-pot some of the vital points in the financial agreement itself. Obviously, therefore, India must provide against strained relations worsening into open breach and thereby, as I was careful to point out in my statement of the 12th December, 'placing all the good work achieved in jeopardy'.

We are, therefore, fully justified in providing against Pakistan's possible continuance of aggressive actions in regard to Kashmir by postponing the implementation of the agreement. We have made it clear to the Pakistan

Government more than once that we stand by the agreement which we reached. The agreement does not bind the Government of India to any fixed date for payment and we cannot reasonably be asked to make a payment of cash balances to Pakistan when an armed conflict with its forces is in progress and threatens to assume an even more dangerous character, which is likely to destroy the whole basis of the financial agreement and would endanger other parts of the agreement, such as arrangements for taking over of debt, and division of stores, etc. The Pakistan Finance Minister claims the amount of Rs. 55 crores as belonging to Pakistan. He has apparently overlooked the fact that on the 14th August 1947, after the Partition Council had decided to allocate the working balance of Rs. 20 crores to the Pakistan Government, the then undivided Government of India issued an order in the following terms to the Reserve Bank:

'Please transfer twenty, half of forty crores, from central closing cash balance on the 14th instant to Pakistan and balance to Indian Dominion as opening balance on the 15th.'

A copy of this telegram was endorsed to the Pakistan wing of the then Finance Department, and no objection was, or has been, raised to this accounting. It follows from this that so far as the bank accounts are concerned, there is no balance of the old undivided Government to be operated upon; the money stands in the name of the Indian Dominion and it is only on the authority of the Indian Dominion that any share can be allocated to the Government of Pakistan.

The relevant portion of the Partition Council minutes also runs thus: 'In addition to the 20 crores, already made over to Pakistan, 55 crores will be allocated to Pakistan in full and final settlement of its claim for a share of the undivided Government's cash balance and of the cash balance investment account.' It is clear, therefore, that nothing belongs to Pakistan until the Government of India transfer the amount to its account. This clear-cut position makes the Pakistan Finance Minister's outburst against the Reserve Bank appear somewhat hysterical and rhetorical. The Reserve Bank cannot do anything without the specific instructions of the Government of India who are the only competent authority to operate the account. He has accused the Government of India of interfering in the discharge of its duties towards the Pakistan Government and has charac-terized this alleged interference not only as an unfriendly act, but as an act of aggression. I wish to say in the most emphatic terms that this accusation is completely baseless and devoid of any element of truth whatsoever. I understand that the Reserve Bank of India first received the demand for the payment of Rs. 55 crores on the 6th of this month in a memorandum handed over to the Deputy Governor of the Reserve Bank at Karachi. I also understand that the Governor to whom this memorandum was telegraphed by the Deputy Governor has sent an appropriate reply. So far as the Government of India are concerned, I would say that when the Reserve Bank mentioned an approach by the Pakistan Government for temporary accommodation from the Bank, the Government of India made it clear to the Bank that it was a matter for the Bank alone to decide. Indeed, the Government of India have made every effort to avoid dragging the Reserve Bank into the controversy. The blame for attempting to force the Reserve Bank into taking sides must rest with the Pakistan Finance Minister. Neither the manner nor the nature of the attempt reflects creditably on the honesty of purpose and the motives of the Pakistan Government.

Gentlemen, I think I have said enough to prove how unfounded and insubstantial are the allegations made by the Pakistan Finance Minister against the Government of India. We have also shown how we have held consistently to the position that the settlement of the financial issues cannot be isolated from that of other vital issues and has to be implemented simultaneously. There can be no question of our repudiating the agreement reached. We only desire that the appropriate atmosphere conditioned by the agreement must be created for its implementation. If the Pakistan Government desires for payment of cash balance in advance, it is obvious that they are motivated by factors wholly opposed to the spirit underlying the agreement. We are thus fully justified in resisting these machinations which, if successful, would vitiate the very basis of the agreement and adversely affect, by facilitating Pakistan's aggressive designs on India, the implementation of other vital parts of the agreement.

GOVERNMENT COMMUNIQUÉ,
THE HINDUSTAN TIMES
16 January 1948

The Government of India have fully clarified their position in regard to the financial settlement arrived at between them and the Government of Pakistan. They have declared that they abide by that settlement, but that the implementation of it, in regard to the cash balances, must be considered as part of an overall settlement of outstanding questions in issue between India and Pakistan. They regret that the Finance Minister of the Pakistan Government should have advanced arguments which are unsupported by facts and which they cannot accept. The factual position has been clearly stated in the statements issued by the Deputy Prime Minister, and the Finance Minister of the Government of India. The facts and arguments contained in these statements represent the deliberate and unanimous opinion of the Cabinet. They regret that the Finance Minister of the Pakistan Government should have again challenged these incontrovertible facts which justify fully the position taken up by the Government of India both on legal and other grounds.

The Government have, however, shared the world-wide anxiety over the fast undertaken by Gandhiji, the Father of the Nation. In common with him they have anxiously searched for ways and means to remove ill will, prejudice and suspicion, which have poisoned the relations between India and Pakistan. Impelled by the earnest desire to help in every way open to them in the object which Gandhiji has at heart, the Government have sought for some tangible and striking contribution to the movement for ending the physical suffering of the nation's soul and to turn the nation's mind from the present distemper, bitterness and suspicion to constructive and creative effort. The Government are anxious to remove as far as possible, without detriment to the national good, every cause, which leads to friction between India and Pakistan.

In view of the appeal made by Gandhiji to the nation, the Government have decided to remove the one cause of suspicion and friction between the two States which, consistently with national honour and interest, it is in their power to remove. They make this spontaneous gesture in the earnest hope that it will be appreciated in the spirit in which it is made and that it will help in producing an atmosphere of goodwill for which Gandhiji is suffering crucifixion of the flesh and thereby lead this great servant of the nation to end his fast and add still further to his unparalleled services to India.

The Government have decided to implement immediately the financial agreement with Pakistan in regard to the cash balances. The amount due to Pakistan on the basis of the agreement, i.e., Rs. 55 crores, minus the expenditure incurred by the Government of India since August 15 on Pakistan account will, therefore, be paid to the Government of Pakistan. The decision is the Government contribution, to the best of its ability, to the non-violent and noble effort made by Gandhiji in accordance with the glorious traditions of this great country, for peace and goodwill.

Part Two

Memorable
Quotations

EFFORT

In my humble opinion, effort is necessary for one's own growth. It has to be irrespective of results.

(Young India, 21 October 1926)

What shall we call 'the best of our ability'? That effort in which a man spends all his energy without stint. Success generally attends such pure effort.

(Bapu-Ke-Ashirvad, 17 April 1945)

HOPE

I never give up hope so long as there is the least chance.

(Young India, 13 July 1921)

HATRED

How can we hate anybody? It is his deeds which we may hate. Hatred of an act elevates our character and that of an individual lowers it.

(Day-To-Day with Gandhi, Vol. II)

HUMILITY

A man who wants to love the whole world, including one who calls himself his enemy, knows how impossible it is to do so in his own strength. He must be as mere dust before he can understand the elements of Ahimsa. He is nothing if he does not daily grow in humility as he grows in love.

(Young India, 25 June 1925)

True humility means most strenuous and constant endeavour, entirely directed towards the service of humanity.

(Yeravda Mandir)

He who is as mere dust of everybody›s feet, is near to God.

(Bapu-Ke-Ashirvad, 10 July 1945)

We are no better than others – this thought is full of truth and humility.

Bapu-Ke-Ashirvad, 12 May 1946)

SIN AND SINNERS

If you have done wrong, whether knowingly or unknowingly, announce it at once and make a resolve not to do it again.

(To Ashram Sisters)

If we repent of our sins, they will not increase further.

(My Philosophy of Life)

What is ' big ' or 'small' in sin? Sin is sin. To believe otherwise, is to delude oneself.

(Bapu-Ke-Ashirvad, 9 August 1946)

None can put him to shame who, of his own free will and even though others know nothing about it, makes a clean breast of his sin and is ashamed of it.

(Bapu-Ke-Ashirvad, 13 November 1945)

SAINTS

I think that the word 'saint' should be ruled out of present life. It is too sacred a word to be lightly applied to anybody, much less to one like myself who claims only to be a humble searcher after Truth, knows his limitations, makes mistakes, never hesitates to admit them when he makes them, and frankly confesses that he, like a scientist, is making experiments about some 'of the eternal verities' of life, but cannot even claim to be a scientist because he can show no tangible proof of scientific accuracy in his methods or such tangible results of his experiments as modern science demands.

(Young India, 12 May 1920)

AHISMA

It seems to me that I understand the ideal of truth better than that of ahimsa, and my experience tells me that if I let go my hold of truth, I shall never be able to solve the riddle of ahimsa .... In other words, perhaps, I have not the courage to follow the straight course. Both at bottom mean one and the same thing, for doubt is invariably the result of want or weakness of faith. 'Lord, give me faith' is, therefore, my prayer day and night.

(An Autobiography)

ECONOMICS

The economics that disregard moral and sentimental considerations are like wax-works that, being life-like, still lack the life of the living flesh.

(Mahatma Gandhiji's Sayings)

PACIFISTS

Pacifists have to prove their faith by resolutely refusing to do anything with war, whether of defence or offence.

(Harijan, 15 April 1939)

ERRORS

He who has no right to err, can never go forward.

(Speeches and Writings of Mahatma Gandhi)

PALATE

Turn to the birds and beasts, and what do you find? They never eat merely to please the palate, they never go on eating till their inside is full to overflowing. And yet, we regard ourselves as superior to the animal creation! Surely, those who spend their days in the worship of the belly, are worse than the birds and beasts.

(The Health Guide)

One who has not been able to control his palate, will never be able to control the other senses.

(My Philosophy of Life)

EATING

There is a great deal of truth in the saying that man becomes what he eats. The grosser the food, the grosser the body.

(*Young India*, 5 August 1933)

If we eat only to sustain the body as an instrument of His service, not only will it make our bodies and minds healthy and clean, but the inner cleanliness will be reflected in our surroundings also.

(Press report, 30 November 1944)

ENJOYMENT

Real enjoyment is derived from drops, not from mouthfuls.

(*The Diary of Mahadev Desai*)

PANIC

Panic is the most demoralizing state anyone can be in. There never is any cause for panic. One must keep heart whatever happens.

(*Harijan*, 8 June 1940)

Panic is the result of fear after all. But a man of prayer knows no fear. Your prayer is vain repetition if it does not clear the atmosphere of fear, panic and mass hysteria.

(*My Philosophy of Life*)

EVIL

Evil has no separate existence at all; it is only good or truth misplaced.

(*Conversations of Gandhiji*)

It is always possible by correct conduct to lessen an evil, and eventually even to bring good out of evil.

(*The Life of Mahatma Gandhi*)

PARENTHOOD

Parents...feel that their children should be educated only in order that they may earn wealth and position. Education and knowledge are thus prostituted and we look in vain for the peace, innocence and bliss that the life of the students ought to be.

(*Young India*, 29 January 1925)

ENMITY

I cannot think of permanent enmity between man and man.

(*Young India*, 2 April 1931)

PASSIONS

A man has first to give up everything that tends to excite or stimulate his passion and then to wait upon God for help.

(Young India, 14 March 1929)

Human passions are fleeter even than the wind, and to subdue them completely requires no end of patience.

(Young India, 27 May 1926)

When your passions threaten to get the better of you, go down on your knees and cry out to God for help.

(Self Restraint V. Self Indulgence)

EQUALITY OF SEXES

Men are equal. For, though they are not of the same age, the same height, the same skin and the same intellect, these inequalities are temporary and superficial; the soul that is hidden beneath this earthy crust, is one and the same for all men and women belonging to all climes.

(Young India, 11 August 1927)

There is as much reason for man to wish that he was born a woman as for woman to do otherwise. But the wish is fruitless. Let us be happy in the state to which we are born, and do the duty for which Nature has destined us.

(Harijan, 24 February 1940)

PASSIVE RESISTANCE

Passive resistance is a method of securing rights by personal suffering: it is the reverse of resistance by arms.

(*Hind Swaraj*)

The spirit of passive resistance rightly understood should make the people fear none and nothing but God.

(*Speeches and Writings of Mahatma Gandhi*)

To become a passive resister is easy enough, but it is also equally difficult. It seems to me that those who want to become passive resisters for the service of the country have to observe chastity, adopt poverty, follow Truth and cultivate fearlessness.

(*The Science of Styagraha*)

SERVICE

A life of service must be one of humility. He who would sacrifice his life for others, has hardly time to reserve for himself a place in the sun.

(*Yeravda Mandir*)

Service is a duty, and duty is a debt which it is a sin not to discharge.

(*Young India*, 28 July 1921)

If we begin to boast of our services to others, or even to feel proud of them, we cease to be moral men.

(*Ethical Religion*)

He who gives all his time to the service of the people, his whole life is an unbroken round of prayer.

(*Harijan*, 10 November 1946)

Remember, that man is a representative of God to serve all that lives and thus to express God's dignity and love. Let service be your sole joy, and you will need no other enjoyment in life.

(*The Health Guide*)

Service which has not the slightest touch of self in it, is itself the highest religion.

(*Harijan*, 25 May 1935)

For real service, what is required is not money but men, men of the right sort with right sentiments, with an abiding love and charity and full of faith in their work. If we do have such men, money will come even unasked.

(*The Hindu*, 27 April 1915)

Social service, to be effective, has to be rendered without noise. It is best performed when the left hand knoweth not what the right is doing. Would that our service were of this nature!

(Service Before Self)

I hold it to be utterly impossible for any young man and any young woman to serve society, unless they start with a clean slate, that is, a pure heart.

(The Hindu, 12 September 1927)

One who serves his neighbour, serves all the world. Indeed, it is the only way open to us of serving the world.

(Ashram Observances in Action)

EQUANIMITY

You must sing and dance with joy in all conditions...You must wear a smile over your face, no matter what comes to pass.

(The Diary of Mahadev Desai)

SILENCE

A sage has said that it is through silence that we become fit for self-realization, and our outer life keeps in tune with the inner.

(Bapu-Ke-Ashirvad, 1 January 1946)

Man spoils matters much more by speech than by silence.

(Bapu-Ke-Ashirvad, 5 February 1946)

The voice of silence has never been denied.

(Harijan, 6 July 1940)

Silence seems difficult. A little practice, however, enables us to like it; and when we like it, it gives us a sense of ineffable peace.

(The Diary of Mahadev Desai)

THE PAST

The past belongs to us, but we do not belong to the past. We belong to the present. We are makers of the future, but we do not belong to the future.

(Bapu-Ke-Ashirvad, 2 November 1945)

THE STRAIGHT PATH

The straight path is as difficult as it is simple. Were it not so, all would follow the straight path.

(Bapu-Ke-Ashirvad, 11 December 1944)

SPEECH

One's speech cannot be judged by one's intentions, but only by the effect it produces on the hearer.

(My Dear Child)

If we stop talking about useless things and talk of things that matter, in as few words as possible, much of our time as well as that of others could be saved.

(Bapu-Ke-Ashirvad, 21 June 1945)

A man of few words will rarely be thoughtless in his speech: he will measure every word. Silence is a great help to a seeker after Truth.

(Thus Spoke Mahatma Gandhi)

HEALTH

No man whose character is not pure can be said to be really healthy. The body which contains a diseased mind can never be anything but diseased.

(The Health Guide)

A pure character is the foundation of health in the real sense of the term, and we say that all evil thoughts and evil passions are but different forms of disease.

(The Health Guide)

PAUPERISM AND PAUPERS

Pauperism must go. But industrialization is no remedy.

(Young India, 7 October 1926)

SELF-DEPENDENCE

Man is born dependent, and dies in dependence. Freedom is a state of the mind. Man is, thus, dependent on others in all things. He is his own master in only a few matters.

(Service Before Self)

PEACE

Though we sing: 'All glory to God on High and on the earth be peace', there seems to be today neither glory to God, nor peace on earth.

(*Young India*, 31 December 1931)

You cannot breed peace out of non-peace. The attempt is like gathering grapes of thorns or figs of thistles. The more I go into the question, the more forcibly the conclusion is borne in upon me that our first duty is to grasp this fundamental fact.

(*Harijan*, 4 June 1938)

Peace has its victories more glorious than those of war.

(*Harijan*, 21 July 1940)

Peace must be just. In order to be that, it must neither be punitive nor vindictive. The strong are never vindictive.

(Press statement, 17 April 1945)

PEACE OF MIND

Each one has to find his peace from within. And peace to be real must be unaffected by outside circumstances.

(*Young India*, 19 November 1929)

Outer peace is useless without inner peace.

(*Bapu-Ke-Ashirvad*, 9 February 1946)

He who lacks peace and firmness cannot realize God.

(*Bapu-Ke-Ashirvad*: 28 May 1946)

HEART

There are chords in every human heart. If we only know how to strike the right chord, we bring out the music.

(*Harijan*, 27 May 1939)

PRACTICE

Indeed, I hold that what cannot be proved in practice, cannot be sound in theory.

(*Wit and Wisdom of Mahatma Gandhi*)

SELF-PURIFICATION

The path of self-purification is hard and steep. To attain to perfect purity one has to become absolutely passion-free in thought, speech and action; to rise above the opposing currents of love and hatred, attachment and repulsion.

(*Young India*, 7 February 1929)

PLAIN SPEAKING

If plain-speaking were rudeness, I am simply saturated with it.

(*Harijan*, 20 April 1935)

SELF-REALIZATION

There can be no realization (of God) without steadfastness of mind.

(*Bapu-Ke-Ashirvad*, 28 January 1946)

The greater man's realization of the Self, the greater his progress.

(*Bapu-Ke-Ashirvad*, 19 September 1937)

Man will ever remain imperfect, and it will always be his part to try to be perfect.

(*Mahatma*, Vol. IV)

No human being is so bad as to be beyond redemption, no human being is so perfect as to warrant his destroying him whom he wrongly considers to be wholly evil.

(*Young India*, 26 March 1931)

TIME

Our time is trust.

(*Young India*, 26 November 1925)

Every minute that runs to waste never returns. Yet, knowing this, how much time do we waste?

(*Bapu-Ke-Ashirvad*, 20 May 1945)

He who wishes to save time will never do a single unnecessary thing.

(*Bapu-Ke-Ashirvad*, 27 July 1946)

Time is a merciless enemy, if it is also a merciful friend and healer.

(*Harijan*, 21 June 1942)

There are things in life for which there is no remedy but time. We have only to allow Nature to perform the healing process.

(*My Dear Child*)

HAUGHTINESS

The man who is proud and haughty may succeed for a while, but he must ultimately suffer.

(*Ethical Religion*)

SELF-HELP

There is no help like self-help. God helps those who help themselves.

(*Harijan*, 5 October 1935)

He who understands the doctrine of self-help blames himself for failure.

(*Young India*, 8 January 1925)

SECRECY

All sins are committed in secrecy. The moment we realise that God witnesses even our thoughts, we shall be free.

(*Young India*, 5 June 1924)

FAITH IN RIGHT

I remain an optimist, not that there is any evidence that I can give that right is going to prosper, but because of my unflinching faith that right must prosper in the end … . Our inspiration can come only from our faith that right must ultimately prevail.

(*Harijan*, 10 December 1938)

Mine is a life full of joy in the midst of incessant work. In not wanting to think of what tomorrow will bring for me, I feel as free as a bird … . The thought that I am ceaselessly and honestly struggling against the requirements of the flesh sustains me.

(*Young India*, 1 October 1925)

Work without faith is like an attempt to reach the bottom of a bottomless pit.

(*Harijan*, 3 October 1936)

EDUCATION

The core of my emphasis is not the occupations, but education through manual training – all education, of Letters, History, Geography, Mathematics, Science etc. through manual training.

(*Harijan*, 30 October 1937)

The school of life is any day superior to the school of books.

(*Harijan*, 18 February 1939)

Experience is the biggest of all schools.

(*Bapu-Ke-Ashirvad*, 2 May 1945)

What we need is educationalists with originality, fired with true zeal, who will think out from day to day what they are going to teach their pupils.

(*The Diary of Mahadev Desai*)

Home life is entirely the sphere of woman and therefore, in domestic affairs, in the upbringing and education of children, women ought to have more knowledge.

(*The Role of Women*)

HONOUR

It is any day better to stand erect with a broken and bandaged head than to crawl on one's belly, in order to be able to save one's head.

(Young India, 2 April 1925)

A keen sense of honour turns every privation into a joy.

(Harijan, 3 February 1940)

SELF

He who realizes not the true wealth that the Self is, nor does he protect it, how can he protect anything else in life?

(Bapu-Ke-Ashirvad, 29 July 1945)**

HELPER

He would be a bad helper who, when hailed to bring a bucketful of water to quench a fire, brought it after even the ashes had been removed.

(Young India, 2 January 1922)**

EXAGGERATION

Exaggeration is also a species of untruth.

(Harijan, 18 March 1933)

It is perhaps human nature to make a mountain out of a mole hill. Only the wise sift the grain from the chaff.

(Harijan, 21 September 1947)

EGO

When the ego dies, the soul awakes.

(Bapu-Ke-Ashirvad, 29 March 1946

While our attachment to the ego remains, we shall never taste the sweet ambrosia of self-knowledge.

(Service Before Self)

How shall we dispel this darkness of egoism? By the light of uttermost humility.

(Bapu-Ke-Ashirvad, 26 July 1945)

A seeker after truth cannot afford to be an egotist. One who would sacrifice his life for others has hardly time to reserve for himself a place in the sun.

(Young India, 16 October 1930)

SHEDDING THE EGO

I know that I have still before me a difficult path to traverse. I must reduce myself to zero. So long as man does not of his own free will put himself last among his fellow-creatures, there is no salvation for him. Ahimsa is the farthest limit of humility.

(*An Autobiography*)

DESTINY

Fates decide my undertakings for me. I never go to see them. They come to me almost in spite of me. That has been my lot all my life long, in South Africa as well as ever since my return to India.

(*Young India*, 7 May 1925)

MY LIFE-CHANGING BOOK

Of these books, the one that brought about an instantaneous and practical transformation in my life was *Unto This Last*. I translated it later into Gujarati, entitling it *Sarvodaya* (the welfare of all). I believe that I discovered some of my deepest convictions reflected in this great book of Ruskin, and that is why it so captivated me and made me transform my life.

(*An Autobiography*)

HONESTY

Honesty from policy is as acceptable as honesty for its own sake. But dishonesty is unacceptable even though it may be actuated by excellent motives.

(*Young India*, 12 January 1927)

SELF-CONFIDENCE

The history of the world is full of instances of men who rose to leadership by sheer force of self-confidence, bravery and tenacity.

(*Mahatma*, Vol. III)

SELF-DEFENCE

A man who is unable to protect himself at a time of crisis is an incomplete man. He is a burden to society.

(*Navajivan*, 29 June 1924)

True self-defence lies along the path of non-retaliation. It may sound paradoxical, but this is what I mean. This would involve suffering. It is this unalloyed suffering which is the truest form of self-defence which knows no surrender.

(*Harijan*, 31 August 1947)

HUSBAND AND WIFE

The very existence of the wife is a great sobering and restraining influence in the life of a married man.

(Day-to-Day with Gandhi, Vol. I)

SALVATION

For me the road to salvation lies through incessant toil in the service of my country and there through of humanity. I want to identify myself with everything that lives.

(Young India, 3 April 1924)

My life is an indivisible whole, and all my activities run into one another; and they all have their rise in my insatiable love of mankind.

(Harijan, 2 March 1934)

A PATIENT

A patient has to eat, sleep, complain and bully. He is an angel when he omits to do the two last things.

(The Diary of Mahadev Desai)

TRUTH

The key to happiness lies in the worship of Truth, which is the giver of all things.

(*Bapu-Ke-Ashirvad*, 7 January 1945)

Why does a person, knowing what is Truth, hesitate to speak it? Is he ashamed? Ashamed of whom? Whether he is a superior or a subordinate, what matters it? The fact is that habit swallows us all. We must reflect over this and rid ourselves of the bad habit.

(*Bapu-Ke-Ashirvad*, 9 January 1945)

Truth should always be accompanied by firmness of purpose.

(*Madras*, 26 January 1946)

To speak the truth, you have to weigh your words again and again.

(*Bapu-Ke-Ashirvad*, 4 June 1946)

When Truth, that is, God, is with us, what matters it if the world is with us or not, and whether we live or die?

(*Bapu-Ke-Ashirvad*. 17 July 1946)

It is million times better to appear untrue before the world than to be untrue to ourselves.

(*Young India*, 6 February 1922)

It is not given to man to know the whole Truth. His duty lies in living up to the Truth as he sees it and, in doing so, to resort to the purest means, i.e. to non-violence.

(Thus Spoke Mahatma Gandhi)

TRUST

I believe in trusting. Trust begets trust. Suspicion is foetid and only stinks. He who trusts, has never yet lost in the world. A suspicious man is lost to himself and the world.

(Young India, 4 June 1925)

I do not trust anybody blindly. But it is our duty to have faith in mankind since we ourselves aspire to other people's confidence.

(Bapu, Vol. I)

Mutual trust and mutual love are no trust and no love. The real love is to love those that hate you, to love your neighbour even though you distrust him. Of what avail is my love, if it be only so long as I trust my friend? Even thieves do that. They become enemies immediately the trust is gone.

(Harijan, 3 March 1946)

Nobody has any right to prejudge anybody. I would trust as I expect to be trusted.

(Harijan, 24 Aug 1947)

PATIENCE

What is patience? Shankaracharya says: 'Sit by the seashore and take one drop of water on blade of grass. If you have enough patience and there is a place nearby wherein that drop can be stored, you may in time empty the ocean of all its water.' This is an illustration of almost perfect patience.

(*Bapu-Ke-Ashirvad*, 25 March 1945)

Even if someone does not listen to what you have told him a hundred times, you must continue with your effort. That is patience.

(*Bapu-Ke-Ashirvad*, 20 July 1946)

When a man's patience is exhausted, he should resort to silence, and speak only when he has calmed down.

(*Bapu-Ke-Ashirvad*, 1933)

THINKING

Our thinking should be aimed at the good of all, and not at satisfying our own selfish desires.

(*Collected Works of Mahatma Gandhi*, Vol. L I. O. 44)

THOUGHTS

Always aim at complete harmony of thought and word and deed. Always aim at purifying your thoughts and everything will be well. There is nothing more potent than thought. Deed follows word and word follows thought. The word is the result of a mighty thought, and where the thought is mighty and pure, the result is always mighty and pure.

(*Harijan*, 24 April 1937)

All thought does not possess the same potency. Only thought, crystallized by a pure life and charged with prayerful concentration, has potency.

(*Harijan*, 6 July 1940)

The Kingdom of Thought knows no boundaries of any kind.

(*Ethical Religion*)

EMPLOYERS AND EMPLOYEES

The relations between the employer and the employee have been up to now merely those of the master and servant, they should be father and children.

(*Young India*, 3 May 1928)

MY FALLIBILITY

I claim to be a simple individual liable to err like any other fellow-mortal. I own, however, that I have humility enough in me to confess my errors and to retrace my steps. I own that I have an immovable faith in God and His goodness, and unconsumable passion for truth and love. But, is that not what every person has latent in him?

(*Young India*, 6 May 1926)

PRACTICAL DREAMER

I believe in absolute oneness of God and, therefore, also of humanity. What though we have many bodies? We have but one soul. The rays of the sun are many through refraction. But they have the same source. I cannot, therefore, detach myself from the wickedest soul (nor may I be denied identity with the most virtuous). Whether, therefore, I will or not, I must involve in my experiment the whole of my kind. Nor can I do without experiment. Life is but an endless series of experiments.

(*Young India*, 25 September 1924)

I must be taken with all my faults. I am a searcher after truth. My experiments I hold to be infinitely more important than the best-equipped Himalayan expeditions.

(*Young India*, 3 December 1925)

It has been my misfortune or good fortune to take the world by surprise. New experiments, or old experiments in new style, must sometimes engender misunderstanding.

(*The Epic Fast*, Pyarelal, Ahmedabad, 1932)

I am indeed a practical dreamer. My dreams are not airy nothings. I want to convert my dreams into realities as far as possible.

(*Harijan*, 17 November 1933)

If any action of mine claimed to be spiritual is proved to be unpractical, it must be pronounced to be a failure. I do believe that the most spiritual act is the most practical in the true sense of the term.

(*Harijan*, 1 July 1939)

ENGLISH LITERATURE

The world is full of many a gem of priceless beauty; but then these gems are not all of English setting. Other languages can well boast of productions of similar excellence; all these should be made available for our common people, and that can only be done if our own learned men will undertake to translate them for us in our own languages.

(*Speeches and Writings of Mahatma Gandhi*)

SACRIFICE

Sacrifice is joy. It is, therefore, not right to parade one's sacrifice before the public.

(*Young India*, 25 June 1925)

There should be no sorrow felt over one's sacrifice. That sacrifice which cause pain, loses its sacred character and will break down under stress. One gives up things that one considers to be injurious and, therefore, there should be pleasure attendant upon the giving up.

(*Young India*, 15 July 1926)

Pure sacrifice is not the thoughtless annihilation of the moth in the flame. Sacrifice, to be effective, must be vacked by the uttermost external and internal purity; without the requisite purity, sacrifice is no better than a desperate self-annihilation devoid of any merit.

(*Harijan*, 8 September 1946)

The law of sacrifice is uniform throughout the world. To be effective, it demands the sacrifice of the bravest and the most spotless.

(*Young India*, 21 April 1930)

HANDWRITING

Handwriting is an art. Every letter must be correctly drawn, as an artist would draw his figures. This can only be done if the boys and girls are first taught elementary drawing.

(*Young India*, 11 July 1929)

HAPPINESS

The briefest and simplest definition of happiness is to live for the happiness of others and to see others happy.

(*The Diary of Mahadev Desai*)

Our happiness and peace of mind lie in our doing what we regard as right and proper, not in doing what others say or do.

(*Bapu-Ke-Ashirvad*, 31 January 1945)

To rejoice in happiness is to invite misery. Real happiness springs from sorrow and suffering.

(*Bapu-Ke-Ashirvad*, 5 May 1945

MY WORK

I shall have to answer my God and my Maker if I give any
one less than his due, but I am sure that He will bless me if
He knows that I gave someone more than his due.

(*Young India*, 10 March 1927)

In spite of my denunciation of British policy and system, I
enjoy the affection of thousands of Englishmen and women,
and in spite of unqualified condemnation of modern mate-
rialistic civilization, the circle of European and American
friends is ever widening. It is again a triumph of non-violence.

(*ibid.*)

PACIFISM

I cannot intentionally hurt anything that lives, much less
fellow-human beings, even though they may do the greatest
wrong to me and mine.

(*Young India*, 12 March 1930)

STRIVING

All have but to do their duty and leave the result in God's
hands. Nothing happens without God's will. Ours is only
to strive.

(*Harijan*, 23 November 1947)

SUCCESS

The true mark of success in life is growth of tenderness and maturity in a man.

(*Bapu-Ke-Ashirvad*, 2 February 1946)

Heroes are made in the hour of defeat. Success is, therefore, well described as a series of glorious defeats.

(*Young India*, 15 January 1925)

HYPOCRISY

Just as we throw away the milk if there is poison in it, so must we reject the good which has got the poison of hypocrisy mixed with it.

(Bapu-Ke-Ashirvad 6 June 1945)

PLEDGES

"Life may perish, but the pledged word may never be broken," (Tulsidas)

(*Bapu-Ke-Ashirvad*, 6 October 1945)

I know that pledges and vows are, and should be, taken on rare occasions. A man who takes a vow every now and then, is sure to stumble.

(*Satyagraha in South Africa*)

SIMPLICITY

There is goodness as well as greatness in simplicity, not in wealth.

(Bapu-Ke-Ashirvad, 31 July 1946)

Simplicity cannot be affected; it should be ingrained in one's nature.

(Bapu-Ke-Ashirvad, 13 April 1946)

PENANCE

We have to cultivate austerity and penance in our life. There is nothing that the power of penance cannot achieve.

(Harijan, 20 October 1946)

Nothing is ever achieved without toil, that is, without Tapa (penance). How, then, can self-purification be possible without it?

(Bapu-Ke-Ashirvad, 17 January 1945)

PLANS

I have found by experience that man makes his plans to be often upset by God; but, at the same time where the ultimate goal is the search of Truth, no matter how a man's plans are frustrated, the issue is never injurious and often better than anticipated.

(*My Experiments with Truth*)

SMILE

Those only can smile well who know how to labour with their hands and feet for others. Those can smile who divide their good fortune with others.

(*Harijan*, 13 February 1937)

THE POOR

The Kingdom of Heaven is for those who are poor in spirit. Let us, therefore, learn at every step to reduce our needs and wants to the terms of the poor and try to be truly poor in spirit.

(*Young India*, 12 January 1928)

✳

PRAYER

Do not worry about the form of prayer. Let it be any form, it should be such as can put us into communion with the Divine. Only, whatever be the form, let not the spirit wander while the words of prayer run on out of your mouth.

(Young India, 23 January 1930)

He who prays from the bottom of his heart, will in time be filled with the spirit of God and become sinless.

(The Diary of Mahadev Desai)

All who flock to churches, temples or mosques, are no scoffers or humbugs. They are honest men and women. For them congregational prayer is like a daily bath, a necessity of their existence.

(Food for the Soul)

Prayer is for remembering God and for purifying the heart and can be offered even when observing silence.

(Harijan, 20 April 1947)

THE POSSIBLE

We can only insist upon what is possible. It is no use pining after the air of the mountains on the moon, as it is beyond our reach.

(The Health Guide)

SUSPICION

The canker of suspicion cannot be cured by arguments or explanations.

(Satyagraha in South Africa)

PRAISE

The best form of praise is to adopt in one's own conduct what one finds praise-worthy in another.

(Harijan, 16 May 1927)

PEOPLE

People are the roots, the State is the fruit. If the roots are sweet, the fruits are bound to be sweet.

(Young India, 2 February 1928)

STRENGTH

When restraint and courtesy are added to strength, the latter becomes irresistible.

(*Young India*, 19 January 1922)

PREACHING

I cannot say what to preach, but I can say that a life of service and uttermost simplicity is the best preaching.

(*Truth is God*)

PREJUDICES

Prejudices cannot be removed by legislation. They will yield only to patient toil and education.

(*Speeches and Writings of Mahatma Gandhi*)

SELF-IMPROVEMENT

Instead of thinking of improving the world, let us concentrate our attention on self-improvement. We can scarcely find out if the world is on the right or wrong path. But if we take the straight and narrow path, we shall find all taking it too, or discover the method of inducing them to take it.

(*The Diary of Mahadev Desai*)

TERRORISM

Terrorise yourself, search within, by all means resist tyranny wherever you find it, by all means resist encroachment upon your liberty, but not by shedding the blood of the tyrant.

(Speeches and Writings of Mahatma Gandhi)

TEXT BOOKS

Less the text books there are, the better it is for the teacher and his pupil

(Harijan, 9 September 1939)

SELF-KNOWLEDGE

Knowledge that sinks deep and becomes part of one's being, is capable of transforming man, provided, however, that such knowledge is self-knowledge.

(Bapu-Ke-Ashirvad, 13 June 1945)

He who does not know himself, is lost.

(Bapu-Ke-Ashirvad, 3 September 1946)

PRINCIPLES

There are eternal principles which admit of no compromise, and one must be prepared to lay down one's life in the practice of them.

(My Philosophy of Life)

The moral principles that are not followed in practice are good for nothing.

(Ethical Religion)

PUBLIC OPINION

Public opinion means the opinion of the society whose good opinion we value, and it is our duty to respect it so long as it is not immoral.

(The Diary of Mahadev Desai)

There is nothing like the growth of enlightened public opinion for eradicating everything evil.

(Young India, 28 April 1937)

TOLERATION

Live and let live or mutual forbearance and toleration is the Law of Life. That is the lesson I have learnt from the Quran, the Bible, the Zend Avesta and the Gita.

(Harijan, 28 October 1939)

Everybody is right from his own standpoint, but it is not possible that everybody is wrong. Hence the necessity of tolerance...Tolerance gives us spiritual insight, which is as far from fanaticism as the north pole from the south.

(Yeravda Mandir)

TRUTH AND NON-VIOLENCE

There can be no comparison between Truth and Non-violence. But such comparison must be instituted, I would say that Truth is superior even to Non-violence. For, untruth is tantamount to violence. The lover of Truth is bound to make a discovery of Non-violence sooner or later.

(The Diary of Mahadev Desai)

There is no such thing as defeat or despair in the dictionary of a man who bases his life on Truth and Non-violence.

(Young India, 31 December 1931)

PUBLIC WORKERS

Public men and public institutions cannot afford to be thin-skinned. They must stand criticism with good grace.

(Young India, 17 May 1926)

TEACHERS

An *acharya* [teacher] is one who behaves himself and thus sets us an example of good behaviour.

(The Diary of Mahadev Desai)

There is no need of a teacher for those who know how to think. The teacher may guide us, but he cannot give us the power of thinking. That is latent in us. Those who are wise, get wise thoughts.

(Speeches and Writings of Mahatma Gandhi)

PUNCTUALITY

If we cultivate the habit of punctuality and acting according to programme, the index of national efficiency will go up, our advance towards our goal will be rapid, and the workers will be healthier and longer lived.

(Teachings of Mahatma Gandhi)

PUNISHMENT

Only he is worthy to mete out punishment whose judgment is infallible. Who but God can be such?

(*Bapu-Ke-Ashirvad*, 24 October 1945)

QUEST FOR TRUTH

Nobody in the world possesses Absolute Truth. This is God's attribute alone. Relative truth is all we know. Therefore, we can only follow the Truth as we see it. Such pursuit of Truth cannot lead anyone astray.

(*Harijan* 2 June 1946)

The instruments for the quest of Truth are as simple as they are difficult. They may appear quite impossible to an arrogant person, and quite possible to an innocent child.

(*My Experiments with Truth*)

When one goes in pursuit of Truth, he finds that it is always eluding his grasp, because he sees now and then that what he once thought too true is no more than fond illusion.

(*Speeches and Writings of Mahatma Gandhi*)

PURITY

All our learning of recitation of the Vedas, correct knowledge of Sanskrit, Latin, Greek and what not, will avail us nothing, if they do not enable us to cultivate absolute purity of heart.

(*Young India*, 8 September 1927)

Your education is absolutely worthless, if it is not built on a solid foundation of truth and purity. If you are not careful about the personal purity of your lives, and if you are not careful about being pure in thought, speech and deed, then you are lost, although you may become perfect, finished scholars.

(*With Gandhiji in Ceylon*)

Truthful dealing even in the least little things of life, is the only secret of pure life.

(*Young India*, 10 December 1925)

Purity asks for no external protection.

(*Harijan*, 9 April 1947)

GOD

The slopes of the Himalayas are white with the bones of our Rishis, who have given their lives to prayer, study and research. They have been trying for centuries to wrest the secrets of God from Him, and what they tell us is: Truth is God, and the way to Him is Non-violence.

(Entertaining Gandhi)

THIEVING

We are not always aware of our real needs, and most of us improperly multiply our wants, and thus unconsciously make thieves of ourselves.

(Yeravda Mandir)

A man who steals and confesses the theft is any day better than a thief who has not been caught as well as the honest man who has never been tempted to steal.

(The Diary of Mahadev Desai)

One man commits a theft, another aids and abets it, while the third only harbours the intention to commit it. All the three are thieves.

(Bapu-Ke-Ashirvad, 2 September 1945)

TAKING

To take what is required may be profitable; to have more given to you is highly likely to be a burden. to overload a stomach is to court slow death.

(*Harijan*, 13 July 1940)

TRUTH AND UNTRUTH

It is million times better to appear untrue before the world than to be untrue to ourselves.

(*Young India*, 6 February 1922)

It is not given to man to know the whole Truth. His duty lies in living up to the Truth as he sees it and, in doing so, to resort to the purest means, i.e. to non-violence.

(*Thus Spoke Mahatma Gandhi*)

TALENTS

Put your talents in the service of the country instead of converting them into pounds, shillings and pence.

(*Young India*, 5 November 1931)

PRIDE

The light of knowledge can never dawn on the proud. Pride of merit damages a soul like a heinous sin.

(*Bapu-Ke-Ashirvad*, 30 August 1946)

BAD TEMPER

Do not lose your temper, if someone calls you a liar or opposes you. If you want to say something, say it calmly. Or, perhaps, silence would be best. If you are really truthful, you do not become a liar simply because someone calls you so.

(*Bapu-Ke-Ashirvad*, 1 July 1945

SORROW AND JOY

Sorrow is but another aspect of joy. Hence, the one invariably follows the other.

(*Bapu-Ke-Ashirvad*, 27 July 1945)

Nanak says: 'The craving for happiness is a veritable disease. Sorrow or suffering is its remedy'.

(*Bapu-Ke-Ashirvad*, 9 August 1945)

Man can smile away his sorrows: by crying he only multiplies them.

(*Bapy-Ke-Ashirvad*, 1 April 1946)

TEMPLES

Temples or mosques or churches... I make no distinction between these different abodes of God. They are what faith has made them. They are an answer to man's craving somehow to reach the Unseen.

(*Harijan*, 18 March 1933)

Our temple is in our hearts. A temple, constructed of a few stones, has no meaning. Only a temple raised in our hearts is useful.

(*To Ashram Sisters*)

Our temples are not meant for show, but for expression of humility and simplicity, which are typical of a devotional mood.

(*Teachings of Mahatma Gandhi*)

ANCIENT TEMPLE TRADITION

I do not hold that everything ancient is good, because it is ancient. I do not advocate surrender of God-given reasoning faculty in the face of ancient tradition. Any tradition, however ancient, if inconsistent with morality, is fit to be banished from the land.

(*Young India*, 22 September 1927)

SUFFERING

It is impossible to do away with the Law of Suffering, which is the one indispensable condition of our being. Progress is to be measured by the amount of suffering undergone. The purer the suffering, the greater is the progress.

(*Young India*, 11 August 1920)

There are limits to the capacity of an individual, and the moment he flatters himself that he can undertake all tasks, God is there to humble his pride.

(*Service Before Self*)

Voluntary suffering is the quickest and the best remedy for the removal of abuses and injustices.

(*Young India*, 29 December 1921)

It would be wrong to brood over the sufferings, to exaggerate them, or to be puffed up with pride. True suffering does not know itself and never calculates. It brings its own joy which surpasses all other joys.

(*Young India*, 19 March 1931)

I want you all to treasure death and suffering more than life and to appreciate their cleansing and purifying character.

(*Young India*, 12 March 1930)

TEMPTATION

We want men and women of grit, immovable faith, and character that will resist temptation.

(*Harijan*, 1 April 1933)

SELF-RESPECT

Dignity of soul and self-respect are interpreted differently by different persons. I am aware that self-respect is often misinterpreted. The over-sensitive man may see disrespect or hurt in almost everything. Such a man does not really understand what self-respect is.

(*Harijan*, 18 August 1940)

SELF-RIGHTEOUSNESS

Many people imagine that they alone are right and everyone else wrong, and they do not consider that there is anything unworthy in forcing their point of view down others' throats. This error has to be rectified. If we are in the right, we must have infinite patience.

(*Harijan*, 28 April 1946)

TEMPLE WORSHIP

Temple worship supplies the felt spiritual want of the human race. It admits of reform. But it will live as long as man lives.

(*Harijan*, 18 March 1933)

EVIL THOUGHTS

Evil thoughts are also a sign of illness. Let us, therefore, guard ourselves against evil thoughts.

(*Bapu-Ke-Ashirvad*, 27 December 1944)

Evil thoughts do not disappear by dwelling upon them, on the contrary, they are likely to become our companions.

(*Bapu-Ke-Ashirvad*, 30 September 1946)

Fight like a lion against wicked thoughts and inclinations. It is our duty to fight, but victory is in God's hands. We must rest content with having striven sincerely.

(*The Diary of Mahadev Desai*)

PRIVILEGES

Privileges may come, as they do come to all, from a due fulfillment of duty.

(*Harijan*, 11 February 1933)

SELF-RULE

He who is unable to rule over himself, can never really succeed in ruling over others.

(Bapu-Ke-Ashirvad, 28 January 1945)

PROGRESS

Men generally hesitate to make a beginning, if they feel that the objective cannot be had in its entirety. Such an attitude of mind is in reality a bar to progress.

(Harijan, 25 August 1940)

Progress is to be measured by the amount of suffering undergone by the sufferer. The purer the suffering, the greater is the progress.

(Young India, 16 June 1920)

In order to make progress, we have often to go beyond the limits of common experience. Great discoveries have been possible only as a result of challenging the common experience or commonly held beliefs.

(My Philosophy of Life)

SOLITUDE

He alone knows the charm of solitude who has deliberately taken to it.

(Bapu-Ke-Ashirvad, July 9 1945)

SPEAKING THE TRUTH

The man of truth is he who will tell and practice the truth, no matter in what circumstances he is placed.

(The Diary of Mahadev Desai)

He who does not know what it is to speak the truth, is like a false coin valueless.

(Young India, 28 April 1920)

Epilogue

A Congressman asked Sri Bhagavan Ramana Maharshi:

… Will India get freedom during Mahatma Gandhi's life time?

Sri Bhagavan … "Gandhiji has surrendered himself to and works accordingly with no self interest. He does not concern himself with the results but accepts them as they turn up …

Follow the example Of Gandhi-ji in the work for the national cause. 'Surrender' is the word".

28 September 1938
(Talks With Ramana Maharshi)